Tactile Strategies for Children Who Have Visual Impairments and Multiple Disabilities

Tactile Strategies for Children Who Have Visual Impairments and Multiple Disabilities:

Promoting Communication and Learning Skills

Deborah Chen

June E. Downing

AFB PRESS

American Foundation for the Blind

Printed in the United States of America

The development of the Project Salute materials was supported in part by the U.S. Department of Education Directed Demonstration Project award #H324T990025 to California State University, Northridge. The opinions expressed do not necessarily reflect those of the U.S. Department of Education, and no official endorsement should be inferred.

Library of Congress Cataloging-in-Publication Data

Chen, Deborah.
  Tactile strategies for children who have visual impairments and multiple disabilities : promoting communication and learning skills / Deborah Chen, June E. Downing.
    p. cm.
  Includes bibliographical references.
  ISBN 0-89128-819-8 (pbk. : alk. paper) — ISBN 0-89128-820-1 (ascii disk)
  1. Children with visual disabilities—Means of communication. 2. Blind-deaf children—Means of communication. 3. Children with visual disabilities—Education. 4. Blind-deaf children—Education. 5. Touch in children. I. Downing, June, 1950- II. Title.

HV1631.5.C44 2006
371.91'1—dc22   2006005010

The American Foundation for the Blind—the organization to which Helen Keller devoted her life—is a national nonprofit devoted to expanding the possibilities for people with vision loss.

It is the policy of the American Foundation for the Blind to use in the first printing of its books acid-free paper that meets the ANSI Z39.48 Standard. The infinity symbol that appears above indicates that the paper in this printing meets that standard.

This work is dedicated to all the families and children who shared their time, efforts, and experiences. Thank you for contributing to an increased understanding of tactile strategies for supporting children with visual impairments and multiple disabilities.

Contents

Acknowledgments

Our sincere gratitude to the children, families, and service providers who participated in Project SALUTE activities. Their participation and input taught us about getting in touch with tactile strategies.

We also extend our appreciation to the members of the project's national advisory committee for their active participation, conscientious commitment, and gentle guidance: Maurice Belote, Julie Bernas-Pierce, Terry Boisot, Jill Brody, Karen Goehl, Eric Kloos, Stephanie MacFarland, Myrna Medina, Barbara Miles, Cyral Miller, Janice Myck-Wayne, Terry Rafalowski Welch, Charity Rowland, Patty Salcedo, Sandy Staples, and Kat Stremel.

In particular, we acknowledge Barbara Miles, Kat Stremel, and Terry Rafalowski Welch for their time, expertise and thoughtful feedback in reviewing the 200+ page manuscript. Their diverse perspectives and helpful suggestions contributed immensely to the organization and content of the manual.

We thank colleagues who shared their insights and wise words about tactile interactions and provided memorable quotes: Maurice Belote, Project Coordinator, California Deaf-Blind Services; Sandy Joint, Statewide Education Advisor (Deaf-Blind), Queensland, Australia; Barbara Miles, consultant, field of deaf-blindness; and Terry Rafalowski Welch, consultant, field of deaf-blindness and Coordinator, Center for Excellence in Augmentative and Alternative Communication, State University of New York at Buffalo.

Kudos to Barbara Porter for her wonderful illustrations that add "life" to our written examples. Special thanks to Mark Schaubert for his technical skills with graphics.

Our appreciation to our project officer Charles Freeman of the U.S. Department of Education for his ongoing support of our efforts.

Special thanks to Natalie Hilzen at AFB Press for her keen eye, fine editing, and suggestions that improved the manuscript, and to Ellen Bilofsky of AFB Press and Jennifer Boeree at Scribe for their work on the production process.

We gratefully acknowledge the many contributions of Project SALUTE research coordinator Lavada Minor, Ph.D., and bilingual coordinator Gloria Rodriguez-Gil. In particular, they both developed the vignettes of Cassandra, Sally, and Manuel and took the photos from which the drawings were made. Lavada Minor contributed to the section on the project's findings in the Introduction and was responsible for writing the section "Considerations for Selecting Strategies" in Chapter 7. Gloria Rodriguez-Gil also contributed to the "Frequently Asked Questions" section in Chapter 7 and to the development of the annotated bibliography in the Resources section and to the definitions in the Glossary.

Lessons Learned from Project SALUTE

Communication is an essential aspect of belonging to a group and participating in everyday life. It is an important skill for all children, but it is particularly critical for children who need supports to learn how to communicate in understandable ways. This manual was written to provide specific information, relevant research, and practical examples that will enhance the efforts of family members and service providers who interact with children who have severe visual impairments and additional significant disabilities, including those with both visual and hearing impairments.

In particular, this chapter offers ways to engage children who do not clearly demonstrate understanding or use of symbolic communication and frequently need tactile information to support their learning. In addition to using tactile strategies to enhance a child's interaction and access to information, interactions should include natural spoken communication as appropriate. Although the content of this manual focuses primarily on using the sense of touch and tactile strategies, a child's use of other sensory avenues needs to be promoted.

Many authors have stressed the use of appropriate visual and auditory input, including suggestions to enhance vision and hearing when either of these distance senses is limited (Downing, 2003; Levack, 1994; Prickett & Welch, 1995). When a child is diagnosed as having a visual impairment and/or hearing loss, he or she needs to receive appropriate services from qualified service providers and adaptive devices (such as hearing aids or other amplification systems and corrective lenses or other magnification systems) as needed. Information needs to be provided through these distance senses whenever possible, and tactile input should be used to support what the child learns through vision and hearing.

Relatively few resources are available to help service providers or family members learn to interact through touch with a child who needs this avenue of information. The information in this manual is designed to address this need. However, all guidelines and suggestions must be adapted to each individual child, family, and situation.

PROJECT SALUTE

The contents of this manual reflect the activities of Project SALUTE (Successful Adaptations for Learning to Use Touch Effectively), a model demonstration project of California State University, Northridge funded by the U.S. Department of Education. The project focused on identifying, developing, and validating tactile instructional strategies for children who have very limited or no functional vision, in addition to hearing loss and cognitive and physical disabilities. We assessed current knowledge about tactile strategies through several methods, including the following:

- An extensive review of the literature

- Interviews with focus groups composed of English-speaking and Spanish-speaking family members and service providers, including individuals who are sighted and visually impaired

- Annual meetings and online discussions with a national advisory committee of experts in the field of visual impairments, severe disabilities, and deaf-blindness who represented family members, service providers, and state and national technical assistance projects

- Input from workshop participants at state and national meetings during the project period

- Reflections on professional experience and practice by project staff

- Interviews with the team of service providers and family members of the four children who participated in the project

- Online postings on the project web site (www.projectsalute.net) in the discussion forum during the project period.

The review of the literature and input from our focus groups and other project participants revealed that tactile strategies used with children who are blind in addition to having multiple disabilities are based primarily on anecdotal reports, opinions, or clinical experiences. The goal of Project SALUTE was to identify, develop, implement, and analyze the use of selected tactile strategies by families and service providers with individual children. In this way we could obtain some data on the effectiveness of particular tactile strategies in meeting the learning and communication needs of individual children.

Focus Group Findings: Practices and Issues

Project SALUTE conducted four focus group meetings in California with 33 participants—English-speaking and Spanish-speaking family members and service providers of children with hearing or vision impairments and additional disabilities. The participants also included three individuals (family members or service providers) with hearing or visual impairments. Researchers asked participants to identify the tactile strategies that they used and to discuss their successes, challenges, and needs. Six themes emerged from this discussion (Chen, Downing, & Rodriguez-Gil, 2000): the need for an individualized approach; meaningful instruction; supportive and positive instruction; a systematic instruction; the challenges of adapting from the visual to the tactile mode; and the difficulties posed by confusing terminology.

Individualized approach. Each child with visual impairments and additional disabilities has unique needs and preferences. Participants stressed the importance of using an individualized approach when determining the best teaching practices and when selecting specific activities and materials. Several reported that children preferred tactile input that had a functional purpose, a simple design, and a concrete form, such as a wooden box with a lid or uncooked beans. Many reported that, in general, children tended to dislike tactile input that was unpredictable, indistinct, complex in form, light, sticky, or extreme in temperature or texture, such as sand, feather dusters, or watercolor paint. On the other hand, a few indicated that their children liked to handle these types of materials. Overall, participants said that they used a trial-and-error approach to determine what worked best for a particular child. They identified a need for the development of guidelines and other tools to help them determine effective tactile strategies.

Meaningful instruction. The importance of meaningful instruction emerged as another overriding theme. Participants felt that children with visual impairments and additional disabilities learn most effectively when instruction occurs within familiar routines, activities, and environments. The use of real items that have a useful purpose, instead of fabricated or artificial ones (for example, a real orange rather than a plastic one) was mentioned repeatedly as essential for enhancing conceptual and language development.

Supportive and positive instruction. The importance of using a positive and respectful approach when interacting with children who have multiple disabilities was also emphasized. Participants felt that children should not be forced to manipulate objects or engage in other tactile learning activities; rather, they should be approached with sensitivity and given ample time to receive tactile information. Repeated use of words such as "rapport building" and "nonintrusive" underscored the importance of this approach.

Awareness of what motivates a child and how to pair that motivation first with familiar and then with unfamiliar tactile items was identified as an effective strategy. The child's individual preferences regarding texture, materials, weight, size, and color need to be considered. For example, some children are motivated by an activity such as music or movement, in which the tactile exploration of objects could be encouraged. Preschoolers who have some hearing and enjoy music may cooperate with handling Play-Doh if the adult sings, "This is the way we roll the Play-Doh, roll the Play-Doh, roll the Play-Doh." The group also stressed consideration for the type of touch and where on the body the child likes to receive tactile information. Instead of demanding that a child hold and examine an item, participants felt that they should follow the child's lead (for example, in the way a child handles or acts on the object), offer opportunities for the child to come into contact with materials, and invite the child to handle items in shared activities (in household tasks or play activities, for example).

Systematic instruction. Participants stressed the importance of routines and repetition to support learning. Consistency in the presentation of information across different settings (such as at home and at school) enables these children to generalize concepts and skills. Children seem to better understand activities with a clearly marked beginning, middle, and end.

Participants also indicated that the use of instructional prompts (such as supporting the child at the wrist to encourage exploration of an object) and cues (such as touching the child's hand with an object) helps children use tactile strategies. Prompts should be withdrawn gradually as the child learns to respond to natural cues.

Challenges of adapting from the visual to the tactile mode. Despite their acknowledged expertise, comments from most participants suggested that adapting visual materials is very challenging. It is difficult to convey adequate information about many concepts or objects through tactile adaptations alone. For example, information about objects that are very large (a car), that are very small (an ant), or that move quickly (a bird flying) requires considerable explanation. Participants indicated that, in these cases, they provided a spoken or signed explanation about the tactile adaptation to the child.

Concepts that are easy to understand when seen are much more difficult to recognize through touch; identifying facial expressions or recognizing feelings is a prime example. The imitation of physical actions is another visually based learning strategy that is difficult to adapt to a tactile mode. Typical tactile adaptations in these situations are to guide the child through specific actions or movements (hand-over-hand guidance) or to let the child feel another person's movements or actions (hand-under-hand guidance). At best, these strategies provide tactile modeling or demonstration. Imitation requires that the child use tactile information to mimic what he or she has experienced.

Although tactile learning often refers to the use of one's hands to learn, focus group participants viewed this as a very narrow interpretation and advocated an expanded definition to include the use of feet, chest, stomach, face, mouth, and the whole body to support children who need to use selected body parts. For example, instead of discouraging a child from mouthing an object, consider whether this may be the most efficient way to gain information for a particular child with significant disabilities. Although these alternative means may be particularly critical for children with significant limitations in use of their hands, participants also indicated that learning through other body parts, such as by examining objects with bare feet, was helpful for children whose hands were hypersensitive to tactile input.

Confusing terminology. Throughout the focus group meetings, participants used many different terms to describe tactile strategies. Some terms, such as *tactile signals, touch cues, motoring, physical prompting,* and *tactile signing,* were defined in different ways. This variation in terms and confusion in terminology also emerged from the literature review. For example, as broadly defined by Rowland and Schweigert (2000), the term "tangible symbols" includes both two- and three-dimensional symbols such as pictures, textures, and objects. However, in the traditional augmentative and alternative communication literature, this same term is restricted to those symbols that can be discriminated on the basis of shape, texture, or other tangible properties, therefore excluding pictures and other two-dimensional symbols (Beukelman & Mirenda, 1998; Downing, 2005a). Similarly, some European authors (Aitken, Buultjens, Clark, Eyre, & Pease, 2000) differentiate between the terms "object cues" and "objects of reference"—a distinction not made in the United States. (See the *Glossary* at the end of this book for definitions of selected terms as used in this manual.) Current dictionaries and the special education literature use the words "tactual" or "tactile" interchangeably; however, in the field of psychophysics, *tactile* refers specifically to information detected through passive touch—contact that is felt as pressure, temperature, or pain—and *tactual* refers to information obtained through active touch—contact involving tactile (cutaneous) sensations and kinesthetic (spatial position and movement) sensitivities (Fleischer & Durlach, 1993). The use of vocabulary from multiple disciplines has produced similar terms with different meanings and multiple terms with similar meanings. For the purpose of simplicity and clarity, this manual will use the word "tactile" to refer to producing a sensation of touch, the capability of being touched, or obtaining information through active touch.

Focus of Project Activities

Based on the literature review and findings of the focus groups, the project encouraged and examined tactile strategies that were based on and supported by social interactions and communication with the four children who participated in the project. The effectiveness of these tactile interactional strategies was measured through the following analyses:

- Videotaped observations of the children in selected activities at home and school were analyzed for changes in the types of tactile strategies that were used by each communication partner, the child's response, and the quality of the interaction.

- Interviews with family members and service providers before and after participation in the project were examined for changes in the types of tactile strategies that were used with the child, the child's response, the context for interactions, and the most frequent communication partners. The post-project interviews also identified positive outcomes for the child.

- Changes on the *Communication Matrix* (Rowland, 1996), which demonstrated the child's type and level of interactions, and the *Home Inventory of Problem Solving Skills* (Rowland & Schweigert, 1997), which identified the child's use of objects, were noted.

Participating Children and their Teams

Tactile strategies were identified, implemented, and evaluated with four children, their families, and their educational teams. Baseline data collection involved observation of activities, interviews, and videotaping of selected activities. Once these data were collected and reviewed, SALUTE staff met with families and educational team members to identify issues, training needs, and goals related to the use of tactile strategies with each individual child, and an action plan was developed with follow-up dates. Project staff disseminated a summary of the meeting and also provided ongoing technical assistance and training as needed. Technical assistance visits involved primarily group discussion and problem solving and, on occasion, modeling strategies with the child and coaching family members and service providers. The level of technical assistance was nonintensive, averaging between three to six visits a year. Some meetings involved the family and team of service providers; other meetings or consultations were held with individual service providers or family members. In the case of three children, their families and service providers requested that the project develop an individualized "communication dictionary" describing touch cues, object cues, and signs to be used with the child. Twice a year, each child was videotaped in selected activities with families and service providers, and these tapes were coded for the families' and service providers' use of tactile strategies and the child's responses.

The project recruited participants through established professional relationships with agencies serving children with hearing and visual impairments in Los Angeles, Orange, and Santa Barbara counties of southern California. To be considered for participation in the project, children had to be labeled as deaf-blind, with little or no functional vision and with additional significant needs (such as motor, cognitive, or health needs), at a nonsymbolic communication level (that is, with no spontaneous use of spoken words or signs), and between the ages of 1 and 10 years old at the beginning of the project. In addition to the families' informed consent granting permission for the project to observe, videotape, and gather other data on their children, families and service providers had to be willing to participate in project activities over the course of 2 years. The goal of the project was to recruit at least four children, with at least one child to represent each age group: early intervention, preschool, elementary, and middle school. As a result of the focus of the project and criteria for participation,

the children who fully participated in the project were boys between the ages of 12 months and 10 years when they first entered the project. Two other children (ages 5 and 9 years), their families, and teachers participated in some aspects of the project but were not involved in our data collection.

Child 1 participated in the project between 12 and 36 months of age. He displayed exploratory behaviors by handling objects; he enjoyed roughhousing games with his brother and father and walking outside with support. He was diagnosed with CHARGE syndrome (a diagnostic label for a pattern of congenital anomalies; see Glossary), had no vision in the right eye, and had a severe visual impairment in the left eye. His hearing loss was severe to profound—90 dB in his left ear and 85 dB in his right ear. Because of feedback from the ear molds of his hearing aids and many ear infections, which required tubes in both ears, he wore the hearing aids inconsistently, and he often pulled them off. He also had a gastrostomy tube and a tracheotomy.

During the first three years of life, Child 1 received weekly home visits from an occupational therapist and an infant development specialist who focused on his vision skills. He also had a health aide at home because of his medical needs. When he was 18 months old, he and his mother attended a weekly center-based program for young children with visual impairments. At first they attended once a week and then increased their participation to twice a week. His parents and service providers were involved in project activities.

Child 1 grasped objects, held them to his left eye, and patted them against his forehead. At age 3, he used body movements and actions on people and objects to request activities (such as a roughhousing game), objects, and attention; and he showed affection, for example, by snuggling into a parent's arms. In addition, at age 3, the communicative meaning of his behaviors was easier to interpret than when he was younger; he had begun to approximate a few signs—like those for MORE and SIT—within context, and he could walk with support. He also had mastered basic skills with objects (approaches, avoids, holds, releases, picks up, bangs, and explores objects; holds two objects and transfers objects from one hand to another) and demonstrated emerging skills in ways to access objects by searching for and locating them. In addition to speaking to the child, his family and service providers provided object cues, some signs on body, and coactive and tactile signs to communicate with him. His family is bilingual (Spanish and English) but speaks primarily English at home.

Child 2 participated in the project between the ages of 4 and 6. During this period, he was in three different classes for children with disabilities in two different school districts. He enjoyed social interactions with his family (particularly with his sister) and other familiar people. He did not demonstrate consistent responses to visual or auditory stimuli. He was nonambulatory and had limited movements, but was able to grasp an adapted cup with both hands and bring the spout to his mouth.

At 6 years old, Child 2 primarily used facial expression and body movements, such as smiling, crying, vocalizing, turning away, or turning toward an object, to request or refuse to do something and to request attention. He would move closer and reach for a desired object, move away from an undesired object, and drop an object with purpose. Also, he was learning to push an easily activated switch with physical assistance to start a cause-effect toy. His family and service providers mainly used object cues and coactive signs in conjunction with speech to communicate with him. Besides having severe hypotonia (very low muscle tone) and developmental disabilities, Child 2 had severe medical needs that have required hospitalization. His family was bilingual (Spanish and English) but spoke primarily Spanish at home. His educational team included a special education teacher, special education assistant, teacher credentialed in visual impairments, teacher credentialed in the area of deaf and hard-of-hearing, an orientation and mobility specialist, and a speech and language therapist.

Child 3 participated in the project when he was between 5 and 7 years old and attended a program for children with visual impairments. He enjoyed being with his family and liked music and banging on the piano. He was totally blind, had a moderate hearing loss, and wore his hearing aids consistently. He was ambulatory and had developmental disabilities and other medical needs. By age 7, Child 3 had expanded his expressive communication to requesting more of an action or object by guiding the adult's hand to an object, using objects to request an action or object, and by signing YES or NO in response to questions offering choices. He also used a few other signs expressively, mainly those relating to foods. He had many basic skills to avoid undesired objects and was mastering skills in ways to gain access to and use objects. His family, which spoke Spanish, and his service providers used object cues and coactive and tactile signs to communicate with him in addition to speech. His educational team included the classroom teacher, one-to-one assistant, occupational therapist, speech and language therapist, and orientation and mobility instructor.

Child 4 participated in the project between the ages of 10 and 12 years and was fully included in his neighborhood schools. He enjoyed social interactions with peers (especially his sister), roughhousing, playing with his dog, and relaxing in the hot tub. Although his visual evaluations and audiological reports showed no visual or auditory responses, his family and service providers indicated that he heard sounds and may have had some functional vision. He wore hearing aids and corrective contact lenses and eyeglasses. Child 4 had developmental disabilities and significant physical disabilities. He was nonambulatory but liked to move as much as his body allowed. He communicated requests for actions, objects, and attention and showed affection through facial expression, body movements, and some vocalizations. To hold objects, he used a palmar grasp—a grasp in which the fingers hold an object in the palm and against the base of thumb. He could transfer an object from one hand to another, activate a switch with physical assistance, and make choices between two items. In addition to speech, his English-speaking family and service providers used object cues, textured symbols, and tactile signs to communicate. His educational team included the general education teacher, special education teacher, one-to-one assistant, teacher in the area of visual impairments, teacher in the area of deaf and hard-of-hearing, and occupational therapist.

Project Findings

Results of the implementation component of this project are limited by the very small number of children and by the heterogeneity of their abilities and needs. All of the children had health and medical concerns, and three of them were hospitalized at least once during the 2 years they participated in the project. Further, two of the children experienced several changes in classes and service providers that required establishing new relationships and refocusing on tactile strategies.

Data analysis of videotaped observations over the course of 2 years reflect the following trends:

1. An increase in the use of appropriate tactile strategies (hand-under-hand guidance, object cues, and adapted signs) by family members and service providers.

2. A decrease in the use of hand-over-hand guidance by family members and service providers.

3. An increase in positive and more active responses from children during interactions, including increased attention to the partner, increased frequency of responses to object cues and signs, and increased frequency of expressive communication. Examples include signing YES when asked WANT EAT; signing MORE to request continuance of a roughhousing game when the adult paused and waited for the child's reaction; holding onto the spoon that was given as an object cue for "time to eat"; indicating a choice between playing and drinking by grasping the relevant object when offered a toy or a carton of juice; indicating a preference for clothing to put on by choosing between two different pairs of pants.

4. An increase in adult's expectation of child's response as measured by an increase in "wait time" and using less support to prompt a response.

5. An increase in readability (clarity) and elaboration (expansions and additional turns) of adults' interactions with children.

Project SALUTE also sought to validate the use of selected tactile strategies with children who are deaf-blind and have significant disabilities. Social validity of an intervention practice involves social acceptance and consideration of the feasibility, desirability, and effectiveness of the intervention procedure (Wolf, 1978) or the compatibility of the intervention with the values and perspectives of families and service providers (Snell, 2003). In other words, are families and service providers able and willing to use tactile strategies, and do these strategies make a difference in communicating with children who are deaf-blind and have additional disabilities? As discussed in Chapter 5, the literature review revealed two studies (Murray-Branch, Udvari-Solner & Bailey, 1991; Rowland & Schweigert, 2000) that found object cues and textured symbols to be an effective communication means for individuals who are deaf-blind with additional disabilities. Although a very small sample, the children in Project SALUTE accepted and benefited from the use of a variety of tactile strategies (mutual tactile attention, tactile modeling, touch and object cues, and adapted signs) that enhanced their social interaction and communication with others.

Family members and service providers of the target children and participants in the focus groups found tactile strategies to be useful and valuable for interacting with and teaching children who are deaf-blind. In follow-up interviews at the end of the project, families of the target children commented on the value of the project in facilitating team collaboration on their child's instruction, improving consistency across environments and people, and providing technical assistance on the use of tactile strategies. Service providers also valued the project's focus on tactile strategies and the opportunities for professional development in working with children who are deaf-blind. They indicated a generalized use of the tactile strategies that they had learned in the project (such as hand-under-hand assistance, object cues, tactile books, and adapted signs) with other children who had visual impairments and additional disabilities. The fact that the intervention procedures developed during Project SALUTE are acceptable to families and service providers is also an indicator of socially valid practices acceptable to families and service providers.

ORGANIZATION OF THIS BOOK

The information contained in this book has been used for workshops with service providers and family members as well as individual and team meetings. In our presentation of the contents, the authors assume that readers have a basic knowledge of ways to support communication with children who have significant and multiple disabilities. Each reader will vary in his or her background and level of skill and knowledge about the use of touch and tactile interaction strategies with children who have multiple disabilities and in his or her purpose for reading the content, and the authors anticipate that most readers will select specific chapters or sections that pertain to their particular concern or question.

Chapter 1, "The Sense of Touch," provides an overview of different types of touch, reminders of varying cultural perspectives, and a comparison of touch and vision. It also offers questions to increase one's awareness of the use and reaction to different types of touch and provides a simulation activity. The next chapter, "Supporting Interactions through Touch," describes the importance of building social relationships, offers suggestions for ways to support a child's use of communication within social interactions, and includes considerations for how and when to use tactile strategies.

Next, Chapter 3, "Assessing Tactile Skills and Planning Interventions," offers a variety of ways of gathering information about a child's use of and experience with touch. The section includes a family interview format, questions for service providers, a sample ecological inventory, discrepancy analyses, and a hierarchy of prompts. Chapter 4, "Focusing on Tactile Strategies," describes the interactional techniques of mutual tactile attention, tactile modeling, hand-under-hand guidance, and hand-over-hand guidance; defines the techniques; and offers considerations for their use, while Chapter 5, "Considering Multiple Communication Options," presents a variety of communication modes, including communication symbols, touch cues, object cues, and textured symbols. Chapter 6, "Adapting Manual Signs to Meet a Child's Needs," describes tactile adaptations to American Sign Language vocabulary, which is a visual system. It addresses the use of signing on a child's body, coactive signing, and tactile signing and offers considerations for their use. Following that, Chapter 7, "Selecting Appropriate Tactile Strategies," addresses the concerns and challenges that may arise when family members and service providers seek to implement the use of tactile strategies. This chapter suggests ways to address these issues and includes frequently asked questions. Chapter 8, "Encouraging Emergent Literacy," highlights the importance of literacy experiences for all children and offers suggestions for supporting initial literacy skills though tactile materials such as experience books and scrapbook boxes.

Finally, the list of resources contains key print and video publications on the topics of tactile strategies and alternative communication modes. It also provides a list of web sites that are relevant to teaching children with multiple disabilities. In addition, the glossary provides definitions of selected terms to assist the reader.

The ultimate goal of this book is to promote improved outcomes in children's communication skills. To this end, the information provided may be used to assist family members and service providers in the development of a child's Individualized Family Service Plan (IFSP) or Individualized Education Program (IEP), particularly in relation to communication needs.

Chapter 1

The Sense of Touch

Touch is perceived through the skin—the largest of all sense organs. Not only is touch the first sense that is developed but also physical contact with others is essential for all aspects of early development (Blackwell, 2000). Consider the significance of skin-to-skin contact on a child's early emotional, social, communicative, and cognitive development. For example, a baby develops a secure attachment with an attentive caregiver who responds to the infant's signals by holding, comforting, feeding, or changing the child. In turn, the infant learns to communicate when crying, smiling, or eye contact elicits the caregiver's physical attention and interaction. When children have visual impairments and other significant disabilities, the sense of touch becomes a critical means of obtaining information about the world around them, communicating and interacting with others, and developing concepts. For this reason, service providers and families of children who are blind should become aware of the importance of the sense of touch and knowledgeable about its vital role in children's learning, growth, and development. This chapter discusses the differences between the senses of touch and vision, cultural influences on the use of these senses, various forms of touch, and research related to the use of touch by children who are blind, including those with additional disabilities. It also provides guiding questions and simulation activities to promote the reader's increased self-awareness and reflection on how he or she uses touch in daily interactions and to enhance the ability to work effectively with children through tactile interactions. When selecting and using tactile strategies with children who are visually impaired and have multiple disabilities, significant differences between the use of touch and vision need to be considered. In addition, selecting and using tactile strategies with these children require careful planning and thought.

The sense of touch is always active because the skin is always in contact with something—another part of the body, clothing, furniture, and so on (Montagu, 1986). In everyday life, it is impossible to eliminate the sense of being touched. Depending on the situation, it may be difficult to differentiate "the sensation of 'touching' from the sensation of 'being touched'" (McLinden & McCall, 2002). In contrast, vision can easily be eliminated by closing your eyes or by turning off the light at night. It is also possible to differentiate between looking at someone and knowing when someone is looking at you.

Vision provides an immediate, holistic, and comprehensive picture of something that is examined (for example, looking at a car), whereas touch provides information on just one aspect at a time (for example, looking at the tires and then the hubcaps and fenders of a car). Compared with visual examination, tactile exploration of an object takes more time and involves the synthesis of a sequence of tactile images to form a complete image of the object.

Touch is a proximal and intimate sense; that is, a person perceives touch only when something or someone comes into actual physical contact with him or her. The term "as far as the eye can see" describes vision as a distance sense, only limited by lighting conditions or a person's visual acuity and range of visual field. Vision is a less "intrusive" sense than touch; although it is socially acceptable to look at people—even strangers—during everyday interactions, it would be inappropriate, bizarre, and even frightening to touch everyone we meet.

Because of limitations in access, distance, size, or safety, not everything that can be seen can be touched. Without vision, a child learns about these types of things through symbolic communication and other experiences. Table 1.1 shows the significant differences between touch and vision that should be considered when interacting with children who have multiple disabilities.

DIVERSE PERSPECTIVES ON TOUCH

A person's views about physical contact and the use of touch are influenced by upbringing, family practices, and cultural values. In some communities, people hug, kiss, hold hands, and touch when interacting with friends and acquaintances. In other societies, this behavior is reserved only for family members (Dresser, 1996). Similarly, in some cultures, people stand very close to one another in conversation, but in other communities, people need at least three feet of personal space (Lynch & Hanson, 2004). Moreover, within each community, the appropriateness of physical contact between people is determined by their relationship, gender, age, and the situation. For example, in contemporary U.S. society, it is socially acceptable for a 6-year-old to sit on her father's lap at home but not at school, and it is acceptable for a 16-year-old to hug her friend when saying goodbye and to wave to her neighbor. In some cultures and religions, it is inappropriate to have any physical contact with nonfamily members of the opposite gender, including shaking hands or using a

TABLE 1.1 DIFFERENCES BETWEEN TOUCH AND VISION AND IMPLICATIONS FOR INTERACTION

Touch	Vision
Proximal sense: Touch requires a child to be in physical contact to maintain interaction with another. The child also needs opportunities to handle and explore materials.	*Distance sense*: Vision requires functional vision, adequate lighting, good contrast, and other ways to encourage vision use. A child can maintain social connection by looking at someone.
Impossible to eliminate: A child has very little control over being touched. He or she may choose not to actively touch or tactilely explore a particular thing, but may be physically guided to do so despite his or her preference. Children who have multiple disabilities are constantly touched during daily care, when handled and positioned; therefore, it is important to interpret and respect the child's responses to being touched or using touch. Also, make sure that specific tactile signals or information is easy for the child to discriminate and recognize from other types of tactile input.	*Can be eliminated*: A child has more control over how, when, and where he or she uses vision. For example, the child can choose whether or not to look at something or may look away or close his or her eyes.
Provides information on one aspect of an object so multiple tactile images have to be synthesized: A child needs time and repeated opportunities to tactilely explore objects and experiences to support integration and understanding of tactile information.	*Provides immediate, holistic information*: A child can quickly look at a visual target and can easily "look again" to check his or her perceptions of the visual information. Vision provides information on size, shape, color, and movement all at once.

human guide or touch cues. Service providers working with children who are visually impaired should discuss with the child's family members the use of tactile strategies to explain their purpose and to determine the family's comfort level with their use for instruction.

Whether certain forms of touch with a child who has multiple disabilities are acceptable to a family may depend on the child's age and the family's culture. For example, massage is a popular practice in some communities. In the United States, massage is a popular means of facilitating a positive emotional bond between a parent and child and supporting this primary relationship during the early years (Schneider, 1996). Infant massage is common in some early intervention programs for children with disabilities (Chen, 1999), though reported therapeutic benefits are yet to be clearly established (Gallagher, 2003). Studies suggest that massage supports positive caregiver-child interactions and may facilitate the child's ability to regulate his or her arousal state (Lappin & Kreschmer, 2005; Pardew & Bunse, 2005). Sensory integration programs may include providing a child with deep pressure touch (such as through a weighted vest) under the guidance of an occupational therapist. Some school-aged students with severe disabilities and medical needs may receive massages for health-related problems, for example, on their feet to aid circulation. However, massage programs for older children with disabilities are not common practice and might be considered quite unusual in schools.

In addition to influences of family upbringing and cultural practices, each person has individual preferences about how he or she likes to be touched. For example, some people like to sit close together, while others need more space between the chairs. Some people enjoy massages, while others do not. Some people like touching slimy things, while others find such textures repulsive. Some people cannot wear certain fabrics because they irritate the skin. A child's individual preferences should be considered when selecting and using tactile strategies to support his or her social interaction and communication.

FORMS OF TOUCH

The literature identifies three different forms of touch (Bushnell & Boudreau, 1991; Heller & Schiff, 1991; McLinden & McCall, 2002; Montagu 1986) that have implications for interacting with children who are blind with additional disabilities:

- *Social touch* promotes attachments and emotional relationships and involves both active and passive touch.

- *Active* or *haptic touch* is the process by which one interacts with the environment and handles and physically explores an object to obtain identifying information that will assist in discriminating and recognizing it. *Active touch* involves information from both the skin's tactile sensations as well as the body's kinesthetic sensitivity to movement and spatial position.

- *Passive touch* occurs when one is touched or one's skin comes into contact with something or someone, and this tactile information is experienced as pressure or temperature that may be unnoticed or may feel soothing, pleasurable, or painful.

Social Touch

Social touch is frequently used in greetings, for leave-taking, to express praise or comfort, and for other social interactions. A child's first experiences with social touch occur during caregiver interactions, early games that involve physical and tactile components (for example, tummy tickling and peek-a-boo), and caregiving routines. The children and families who participated in Project SALUTE had developed various tactile interaction games that delighted all participants: "crunchy ice-lemonade," a pat-a-cake-like clapping game; "timber," in which soft stuffed animals are dumped over the child; and "doggy kiss," in which the family dog licks the child's face. Social touch involves both active touch (in which the child touches another person) and passive touch (in which the child is touched by another). Examples of social touch in which the child is passive include receiving a massage, having his or her hair combed, or getting a hug. Examples of social touch in which the child is active include patting a friend's hand, hugging a parent or other caregiver, or combing a sibling's hair.

Children who are visually impaired with multiple disabilities may need additional ways to maintain social relationships with family, friends, and service providers through social touch. Each communication partner should be sensitive to the child's likes, dislikes, and personal preferences regarding touch. As discussed, one's culture and values influence the types of tactile interactions that are considered socially acceptable. Some service providers may be hesitant to interact tactilely with a student of the opposite gender because of cultural differences or a fear that tactile interactions may be misinterpreted as inappropriate. Some families may be concerned about the use of touch cues or adaptive manual signs with their children, particularly by nonfamily members.

Educational programs may have policy guidelines regarding the types of social touch that are appropriate between males and females. Program administrators, service providers, family members, and the student (as appropriate) should discuss the use of social touch, particularly when children are visually impaired, and caregivers should gather information about the child's preferences through conversations with the family, careful observations, and planned interactions. (To learn more about cultural influences on social interactions including touch, see Dresser, 1996; Lynch & Hanson, 2004 and the Culturally and Linguistically Appropriate Services web site at http://clas.uiuc.edu in the Resources section.)

A process of self-reflection is needed to recognize one's own use of physical contact and reactions to tactile interaction. Remember that each person who interacts with a child is communicating not only the obvious message through words, gestures, signs, and other communication means but is also conveying hidden messages that may be emotional, including feelings about the child, the activity, and one's own ability and interest in interacting with the child. To increase self-awareness about social touch, consider the following questions:

1. How do I physically interact with family members and close friends (for example, by hugging, kissing, holding hands, patting on the back)? How do they respond?

2. How do I physically interact with acquaintances (for example, by shaking hands, patting on the back)? How do they respond?

3. How do I physically interact with children in the family or children of friends (for example, by hugging, kissing, holding hands, patting on the back, showing them something)? How do they respond?

4. What types of physical contact do I like or dislike (for example, massage, deep pressure, light touch, pats on the back)?

5. How do I respond to physical interactions (for example, when someone else touches me to get my attention)?

6. How do I obtain information about the preferences of students who are visually impaired regarding physical contact and tactile input?

7. How do I physically interact with my students who are visually impaired (for example, to greet them, get their attention, show them something)?

8. Do my hands invite the child to interact tactilely? Are they accessible, relaxed, pleasant to touch, and responsive?

9. How do I express different feelings through my touch (for example, when I'm happy, upset, tired, resistant, disapproving)?

Also consider the following questions to guide your observations of a child's responses to social touch:

1. Who engages in physical interactions (for example, touching, hugging, patting on the back, roughhousing) with the child? When do these interactions occur?

2. How does the child respond to these interactions?

3. Does the child initiate physical social contact with others (for example, through reaching out to touch, hug, or pat someone)?

Children who are blind use both social and active touch during social interactions to enable them to recognize significant caregivers and to discriminate them from other people. Fraiberg (1977) observed that infants who are blind increased their manual tactile exploration of their mother's face between 5 and 8 months of age and demonstrated discrimination in their responses to being held by their mother or strangers.

In a review of the literature on the development of infants with visual impairments, Warren (1994) identified the types of tactile stimuli that elicited responses from these infants during the first year and how the infants responded. He found that 2-month-old babies actively sought tactile contact with their mothers and smiled in response to this contact. Four-month-old babies touched their mothers' noses and grunted and moved a pacifier from hand to

hand and from hand to mouth. Five-month-old infants grasped or mouthed a plastic rattle and tactilely explored the parent's face with their hands. Six-month-old infants smiled when tickled on the chest. Seven-month-old infants searched, found, and mouthed a cookie they had dropped; quieted and touched the mother's face when held by the mother; squirmed, wiggled, and cried when held by a stranger; searched randomly for a dropped toy; and grasped a toy that touched the back of their hands.

Active Touch

A child requires some degree of motor control in his or her arms, hands, and fingers, or feet to be able to handle and examine objects or people without assistance, that is, to use *active touch*. To obtain useful information about what is being examined, this child needs to employ a variety of exploratory behaviors. With the exception of Fraiberg's early observations (1968, 1977) of infants' tactile interactions with caregivers, the literature has focused on the use of active touch related to the examination of objects. Between 4 and 6 months of age, sighted infants tend to increase their use of active exploratory movements by using one hand to manipulate and examine objects (Morange-Majoux, Cougnot & Bloch, 1997). As early as 6 months, sighted infants' exploratory actions are related to the properties of objects (for example, shaking a bell, banging an object on a hard surface, squeezing a sponge) (Palmer, 1989; Ruff, 1984). Certain characteristics of objects attract the child's tactile examination. Nielsen (1991) found that young children with visual impairments and additional disabilities spent more time handling objects that had varying tactile characteristics (for example, materials that varied in material, size, and shape, such as rattles and rubber pads) and compared details in their handling of objects when they were moderately different in tactile qualities (for example, objects of similar material, size, or shape, such as metal spoons and keys).

Several studies have examined the characteristics of the exploratory behaviors used by infants who are visually impaired. Some investigators have focused on the differences in infants' responses to novel and familiar objects, and others have examined the types of behaviors that infants use to explore objects. One study with two infants with low vision who were 6 to 10 months of age suggested that infants in this age group demonstrate memory of shapes and texture perceived tactilely by a lower level of manipulation of familiar objects and higher level of manipulation of novel objects (Catherwood, Drew, Hein & Grainger, 1998). Another study (Schellingerhout, Smithsman & Van Galen, 1998) found that eight infants (9 to 22 months of age) who were congenitally blind with no additional disabilities began

fingering at a later age (13 months) than sighted infants (5 months) (Ruff, Saltarelli, Capozoli & Dubiner, 1992). Observations of infants who were blind suggest the following developmental trends (Schellingerhout et al., 1998):

- *8 months*: mouthing and grasping

- *13 months*: mouthing and examining through differentiated hand and finger movements (manual exploration)

- *22 months*: manual exploration

Bradley-Johnson and her colleagues (2004) examined the use of 12 exploratory behaviors of infants between 12 and 23 months who were blind and those who were sighted. These exploratory behaviors included mouthing, using the face area, pushing, shaking, making hands-on contact, rotating, squeezing, fingering, banging, transferring hand to hand, pulling apart, and dropping, throwing, or pushing away. Like Schellingerhout and his colleagues (1997, 1998), they found that both groups used a variety of exploratory behaviors that fit the properties of selected objects (for example, shaking a rattle and pushing a car). Little evidence of mouthing was found in 1- to 2-year-old infants who were blind (Bradley-Johnson et al., 2004). In contrast, Schellingerhout and colleagues (1997) found that infants who were sighted tended to decrease mouthing by the end of the first year, but this decrease did not occur as early in infants who were blind. These researchers suggest that infants who are blind may use mouthing because they focus on different characteristics of an object or use oral-manual inspection because they do not have access to manual-visual exploration.

Children with visual impairments and additional disabilities have been reported to demonstrate decreased manual exploration skills in comparison to sighted children without disabilities. Rogow (1987) found a relationship between language levels and the ability to manipulate objects in 148 children and adolescents ranging from 3 to 19 years of age who were blind or visually impaired. The individuals who had limited or no speech skills tended to have limited hand function and were more likely to have unusual or stereotypical hand mannerisms. In comparison, individuals who had age-appropriate speech and language abilities demonstrated exploratory behavior and object play and no stereotypical mannerisms.

Recently, McLinden (1999, 2004) examined the haptic (active touch) behaviors of nine children between the ages of 3 and 15 with severe visual impairments and additional disabilities. He found a range of behaviors during their interactions with objects—reaching, grasping, holding, transferring, and using hands and mouths—but not all children demonstrated all behaviors. Some of these behaviors were similar to certain "exploratory procedures" (Lederman & Klatsky, 1987):

1. *Lateral motion*—rubbing the fingers across the surface of an object

2. *Pressure*—squeezing or poking an object

3. *Static contact*—holding the fingers static on the surface of an object

4. *Enclosure*—holding or grasping an object with the hand

5. *Unsupported holding*—holding an object unsupported in the hand

6. *Contour following*—tracing the contours of an object with the fingers

[McLinden, 2004]

Although some of the actions demonstrated by children with visual impairments and additional disabilities were different in appearance, McLinden (2004) suggests that these actions may have similar functions (that is, to gather information about the qualities of the object):

- *Lateral motion*—rubbing object on lip or cheek, scratching with fingernail, licking object

- *Pressure*—biting, tapping, or patting object, tapping or patting object on body part

- *Static contact*—holding an object against body part

- *Enclosure*—putting object in mouth

- *Unsupported holding*—balancing object on head

- *Contour following*—rubbing object across the face or body

According to McLinden, systematic observation of a child's haptic movements of different objects can reveal the child's range of exploratory movements. In turn, this information may be used to offer experiences that will support the child's understanding of objects.

Almost 30 years ago, based on the research literature on tactile discrimination in sighted children, Barraga (1986) suggested a possible developmental sequence for tactile-kinesthetic perception in children who are blind:

1. *Awareness and attention* to materials with different textures, temperatures, and vibrating surfaces

2. Discrimination of *structure and shape* of different types and sizes of objects through grasp and manipulation

3. Recognition of *relationship of parts to the whole* through taking apart and putting together a variety of objects during play

4. Recognition of *graphic representations* requiring a high level of tactile perception and cognitive association as flat two-dimensional forms do not resemble their three-dimensional referents

5. Recognition of *braille* requiring a level of tactile perception and cognitive association similar to visual recognition of print letters and words

This framework continues to provide a guideline for the development of tactile and early literacy experiences for children who are blind and have additional disabilities. To help identify opportunities for active touch, consider the following questions:

1. When can the child be encouraged to handle and tactilely examine materials during daily activities?

2. What types of materials (for example, function, size, shape, texture, composition) are likely to motivate the child's tactile exploration?

3. What types of supports does the child need to examine materials tactilely?

Research (Gibson, 1962, 1966) suggests that *active touch* using exploratory procedures to examine objects provides more information than *passive touch*. Others have suggested that both types of touch are used in daily exploration and that the efficacy of *active* over *passive* touch may depend on the type of object being examined and whether one is familiar with this object. For example, a reader using an electronic braillewriter keeps his or her finger over a single "refreshable" braille cell display in which letters are raised in sequence (McLinden & McCall, 2002). The movement of the object touching the person's hand appears to be the critical feature. In his experiments on passive touch, Gibson (1962) found that moving an object provided more information than merely placing the object on the person's hand.

Passive Touch

Children who are visually impaired with significant and additional disabilities frequently experience *passive touch* during routine medical interventions, daily care, and in use of physical prompts (such as hand-over-hand guidance). They may have little experience with *active touch*, unless family and service providers provide specific opportunities and the necessary support and time for these children to develop and use tactile exploratory strategies. In many cases, children with visual impairments and additional disabilities require assistance to manipulate and explore objects. Such exploration may be particularly difficult for children with significant motor difficulties. All too often, individuals interacting with a child who has multiple disabilities may resort to physical manipulation of the child's hand over objects and other tactile stimuli contributing to an abundance of *passive-touch* experiences. If touch is a primary mode of receiving information for a particular child, then a distinction should be made between opportunities for *active-* and *passive-*touch experiences.

As illustrated in Table 1.2, a child's reaction to and use of social, active, and passive touch can be identified. This type of summary enables the development of suggestions for using tactile strategies within the child's everyday activities.

SENSORY INTEGRATION

Some children who have multiple disabilities and visual impairments demonstrate certain behaviors that may be related to sensory modulation problems (difficulty managing reactions to sensory input). Children with these problems may appear to be hyperreactive (having a low threshold of arousal so they are easily overwhelmed by sensory input); sensory avoidant (having a low threshold of arousal so they actively avoid sensory input); hyporeactive (having a high threshold of arousal so they require increased sensory input); or sensory seeking (having a high threshold of arousal so they actively seek sensory input) (Williamson & Anazalone, 2001). For example, one child may avoid touching or

TABLE 1.2 SUMMARY OF CHILD'S USE OF TOUCH

Name: <u>Leon S.</u>　　　　　　　　　　Age: <u>8 years</u>

　　　<u>McKinley Elementary School</u>　　Date: <u>3/20/06</u>

Informants: <u>Mrs S. and Teacher</u>

Type of touch	Response and use	Likes
Social touch	Attends to social touch (for example, greetings, physical praise) but may not actively respond Sometimes smiles when someone tries to engage him in physical play (for example, hand-clapping games)	Engages in physical play with his mother and sister Accepts social touch from familiar and unfamiliar people
Active touch	Independently reaches for food or favorite toys Searches for objects in schedule box when prompted Reaches out to touch familiar people for attention or interaction	Enjoys smooth objects that vibrate (for example a rubber band that he vibrates near his ear)
Passive touch	Allows hand-over-hand assistance Holds object with light grasp but seldom initiates exploration	Sometimes waits for mother to manipulate his hands to prompt him to continue an action (for example, washing hands)

Dislikes	Strengths	Needs and suggestions
Dislikes abrupt or rough interactions with people (for example, rough play with his uncle)	Seeks social interaction with family members (for example, hugs mother, makes physical contact with sister, searches for father) Plays and interacts with family members	Use mutual tactile attention to increase social interactions* Do activities together; encourage Leon to feel what you are doing (for example, eating the same snack at the same time) Use tactile modeling to demonstrate how to respond socially to others (for example, greeting, giving and receiving objects)*
Has an aversion to wet, sticky materials	Interested in exploring environment when looking for favorite toy or food	Continue offering choices between two or three items Encourage active touch by creating an environment that is tactually interesting Engage a peer in tactile modeling of activities with Leon
Rejects hand-over-hand assistance if he doesn't like the activity	Responds appropriately with a minimal prompt most of the time	Continue decreasing hand-over-hand assistance by using elbow or wrist prompt

* See Chapter 4.

handling particular textures (sensory avoidant), and another may persist in mouthing certain objects (sensory seeking). The interdisciplinary perspectives of professionals with expertise in sensory integration, functional behavioral analysis, communication, visual impairments, and severe disabilities—as well as the input of the child's family—may be required to help in the examination of these types of behaviors. A comprehensive discussion of sensory integration and sensory processing is beyond the scope of this book; however, this section will introduce a few basic concepts to encourage interdisciplinary collaboration in analyzing the complexity of a child's puzzling behaviors.

Sensory integration refers to the organization or processing of sensory information (Williamson & Anazalone, 2001). It focuses on the individual's responses to input from the "near senses"—tactile, vestibular, and proprioceptive (Lynch & Simpson, 2004). From a sensory processing perspective, differences in children's reactions to sensory stimuli are related to the differences in their sensory thresholds.

Experts in sensory integration (Dunn 1997; Williamson & Anzalone, 2001) conceptualize the sensory threshold as a continuum. At one extreme, a low threshold indicates an increased sensitivity; at the other, a high threshold is marked by a decreased sensitivity to stimulation. A child who has a low sensory threshold will appear hyperreactive to certain sensory input, may seek to avoid sensation, and may be easily overstimulated. Firm touch may calm this child (Lynch & Simpson, 2004). A child with a low sensory threshold needs a quiet, very predictable, and organized environment with opportunities to "take a break" from ongoing activities. In contrast, a child who has a high sensory threshold will be hyporeactive to sensory stimuli, may seek sensory input, and will need stimulation to be attentive and alert. This child needs short activities involving art and manipulative materials, and physical and movement activities. Children who demonstrate undersensitivity to stimulation may appear passive and tired but become more interactive after vigorous physical play. Some children may seem inconsistent in their responses to sensory stimulation because of multiple influences, including the environment; the child's level of arousal, emotional state, accumulated sensory build-up; and the presence or absence of a familiar person (Williamson & Anzalone, 2001). Questions and concerns about an individual child's unusual responses to tactile input should be addressed to the child's occupational therapist, who should have a background in sensory integration.

SIMULATION ACTIVITIES

Participation in simulation activities promotes opportunities for family members, service providers, and peers to experience the child's point of view and to practice providing and receiving tactile information. Simulation Activity 1 is an activity that involves the identification of objects through active touch, Simulation Activity 2 illustrates ways to identify touch-related preferences, and Simulation Activity 3 offers insight into communicating through touch.

Simulation Activity 1: Identifying Objects through Active Touch

1. Gather a variety of materials (for example, real and artificial fruit and vegetables, miniatures, or decorative replicas of objects) in a bag.

2. Ask for two volunteers to close their eyes.

3. Hold up the materials and ask the other participants to look at them without labeling the items aloud.

4. Give the materials to the volunteers and ask them to identify them through tactile examination.

5. Ask the volunteers to open their eyes and discuss what characteristics made the objects easy or difficult to identify (for example, familiarity, size, texture, weight, material, smell, movable parts, etc.) Based on this experience, discuss types of objects that are the easiest to identify (for example, real objects,

items within the experience or knowledge of the person) and characteristics of those that are more abstract and are more difficult to recognize tactilely (for example, models or artificial representations, unfamiliar items) and require language and a variety of experiences.

6. Discuss the difference between gathering information through vision and through touch and the implications for the instruction of children who are visually impaired and have additional disabilities: for example, select and introduce objects for the child to touch carefully; observe and respect the child's response to tactile materials; allow sufficient time for the child to explore the materials; and provide repeated opportunities for the child to touch and handle the object.

Simulation Activity 2: Identifying Preferences Related to Type of Touch

1. Pair up with another person to simulate adult-child pairs.

2. Do not communicate through speech or sign.

3. The "adult" is sighted; the "child" should close his or her eyes to simulate vision loss.

4. The "adult" should touch the "child" first using a soft/feathery touch and stroke, then using a firm touch and stroke.

5. Switch roles.

6. Discuss feelings and preferences regarding the types of touch.

Simulation Activity 3: Communicating through Touch

Plan this simulation activity by making the directions available for the group and writing the tactile "messages" on two different-colored index cards to be distributed to each pair. Neither person should see the other's card because the goal of the activity is to communicate tactilely the message on the card.

1. Pair up with another person to simulate interacting with a child who is blind.

2. One person is sighted; the person playing the role of the child closes his or her eyes.

3. The "sighted person" does not speak and touches the "child" to express the following messages:

   • Greeting ("Hi, I'm here.")

   • Disapproval ("Stop that, now!")

4. The "child" responds to indicate whether or not he or she understands the message.

5. Switch roles.

6. The "sighted person" does not speak and touches the "child" to express these messages:

   • Direction ("Let's sit here.")

   • Praise ("Wow, you did a great job!")

7. The "child" responds to the message that he or she perceives.

8. After everyone has had a turn being the "child," ask what made the message easy or difficult to express or understand. Have the group reflect on the experience and share their reactions and insights.

The meaning of communication is supported by the context in which it occurs. Because the communication in Simulation Activity 3 is "out of context," it highlights the need for the sender to make the meaning of the message clear to the receiver—that is, a child who does not understand symbolic communication—by providing routines, nonsymbolic communication means, objects, and other cues that enhance understanding, as in the following example:

1. The greeting, "Hi, I'm here," indicates that a familiar person has just returned to the receiver and that the receiver is aware of this occurrence.

2. The direction, "Stop that, now," assumes that the receiver is engaged in doing something that is disliked or not allowed by the sender and can relate this prohibition to a specific behavior.

3. The suggestion, "Let's sit here," assumes that the sender and receiver are standing and looking for a place to sit.

4. The comment, "Wow, you did a great job," indicates that the sender is pleased with something that the receiver did and that the receiver can relate this praise to a specific action.

These types of simulation activities may be repeated to convey different messages by practicing the following tactile strategies, which will be discussed in subsequent chapters:

- hand-over-hand guidance

- hand-under-hand guidance

- tactile modeling

- mutual tactile attention

- sign on body

- coactive signing

- tactile signing

Simulations are also useful when planning tactile adaptations to activities and materials for an individual child. Opportunities to experience what this child will encounter will provide both adults and peers with a valuable perspective to support their interactions with the child who needs tactile information.

SUMMARY

This chapter has provided an overview of the sense of touch as a means of interacting and gaining information. Relevant research and different types of touch—social, active, and passive—were discussed along with ways to encourage a child's use of diverse tactile input. Simulation activities were suggested to increase a communication partner's awareness of how he or she uses different types of touch. The sense of touch is an essential avenue of information for the child who is blind with additional complex disabilities; therefore, those supporting the child's development will need to become familiar with this sensory mode.

Chapter 2

Supporting Interactions through Touch

In the absence of the ability to use vision or hearing as a means to obtain information, communicate, and interact with others, a child's use of touch must be developed, supported, and refined. Tactile strategies need to support natural social interactions and conversations through symbolic and nonsymbolic means. It is best if the use of selected tactile communication modes specifically meets the communication needs of an individual child and supplements the child's body language and other means of communication. Just as hearing children are exposed to thousands of words before they begin to talk, children who are visually impaired and have multiple disabilities need consistent and extensive experience with objects, signs, and other symbols during natural, everyday situations before they can understand their meaning. Besides tactile communication strategies, communication partners may use speech, gestures, and other natural means of communication to encourage natural social interactions with the child who has multiple disabilities and as a means to provide additional communicative information to a child who has some functional vision and or hearing. Turn-taking and conversational exchange are the basis of communication and language learning, and children with sensory impairments and multiple disabilities require specific supports to develop and participate in early turn-taking games and conversations (Klein, Chen & Haney, 2000; Miles & Riggio, 1999). As Table 2.1 demonstrates, tactile strategies have certain benefits for children with visual impairments and multiple disabilities as well as their communication partners.

Various communication modes for children with sensory impairments and multiple disabilities, which are listed in "Modes of Tactile Communication," will be described in the chapters that follow, along with essential principles of communication. This chapter offers suggestions and helpful guidelines on ways to communicate effectively with children who benefit from the use of tactile means and to support their development of receptive and expressive communication or the reception and expression of a message with another.

GENERAL TIPS FOR TACTILE INTERACTIONS

When interacting with a child with sensory impairments and other disabilities, consider the following general interaction tips:

- Greet the child by touching the back of his or her hand or shoulder.

- Introduce yourself by saying your name and identifying yourself tactilely (for example, use a name sign, object, or identification cue).

- Maintain contact with the child by sitting where you can see the child's responses and where you are available as a communication partner. Offer your hand to the child (for example, under the child's hands so the child can grasp your fingers or get your attention) or place your hand or hands beside or slightly underneath the child's hands or a part of the body that is engaged in this activity or movement.

- Expect a response and wait for it.

TABLE 2.1 BENEFITS OF TACTILE STRATEGIES	
For a child who is visually impaired	**For the child's communication partners**
• Addresses an important sensory mode • Helps the child to anticipate familiar events • Directs the child's attention to ongoing activity • Increases opportunities for social interaction • Supports participation in activities • Gives meaning to activities • Supports receptive and expressive communication	• Encourages thoughtful and organized interaction with the child • Increases observations and responses to the child • Promotes an expectation of the child's response • Supports communication that is accessible to the child

When interacting with a child, let him or her know that you expect a response by touching the child to indicate that it is his or her turn or by pausing after you initiate an interaction.

• Make sure the child knows that you are there—through physical contact, if needed—and wait for a response. Allow the child to indicate a message in some way (for example, by a movement, a touch, or vocalization), and then respond in a way that is meaningful to the child. Engage in these interactions as often as possible throughout each day. Avoid "doing something to" or for the child without the child first asking for your assistance or without asking for the child's consent to your assistance.

• Encourage the child to explore the environment tactilely (for example, to examine materials on the table, to feel your hands while engaged in a variety of activities, or to examine the activities of others).

• Place your hands under the child's hands as you explore together.

• Make your hands available to the child by resting them quietly beside

---

MODES OF TACTILE COMMUNICATION

Touch cue: A physical prompt made in a consistent manner directly on the body to communicate with a child

Object cue: An object or part of an object used to represent a person, place, object, or activity. This object may be used in the actual situation

Signs on body: A standard manual sign that a signer produces directly onto the receiver's body

Coactive signing: Physical guidance of a child's hand or hands to facilitate production of a standard manual sign for expressive communication

Tactile signing: Communication method based on a standard manual sign system in which the receiver's hand or hands are placed lightly upon the hand or hands of the signer to perceive the signs tactilely

and just touching the child's hands. Spend time with the child and focus on interaction without preconceived performance expectations. Let the child know that you are present. Keep your hands calm, relaxed, and accessible. Look at the child's hands, face, and body and interpret his or her expressions and movements. Wait and let the child initiate and reach out to you.

- Keep "in touch" with the child during shared activities so that he or she knows that you are both engaged in the activity together. For example, when doing an activity at a table, maintain contact with the child by making your hands available to his or hers or by gently touching elbows so the child knows that you are there. Figure 2.1 illustrates "keeping in touch" while going down the slide together.

- Develop tactile turn-taking games by touching the child and encouraging a response (for example, pat the child's fingers and then wait for the child to wiggle his or her fingers or pat yours).

- Encourage a variety of communicative functions in the conversation (for example, requesting, rejecting, commenting, and getting attention) and respond appropriately. For

instance, "interrupt" a familiar activity (playing with a vibrating pillow) by stopping the activity (turning off the pillow) and wait for the child to "request" more of the activity (for example, by patting the pillow or signing ON or MORE) before continuing the activity. Set up a favorite activity (a snack) but do not begin it; wait for the child to get your attention (by vocalizing, patting the table, or signing EAT) to initiate

Figure 2.1 Keeping in touch: Going down slide

the activity. Offer the child a low-preference food or toy so that he or she will reject or refuse it by pushing away, shaking his or her head, or signing NO.

- Encourage "tactile conversations" about things by touching them jointly with the child. Explore objects together. For an illustration, see Figures 2.2 and 2.3, which demonstrate a conversation about an orange.

- At the end of an activity or interaction with objects, let the child know that the activity is over (for example, sign FINISH), and tactilely model for the child how to put objects in a box or push them away.

- Say goodbye before leaving the child by using a goodbye gesture (for example, wave or use a touch cue on the shoulder) and having the child tactilely attend to this signal.

RESPONDING TO THE CHILD'S PREFERENCES AND ACTIONS

Keep in mind the following tips to guide your interpretation of the child's preferences and actions:

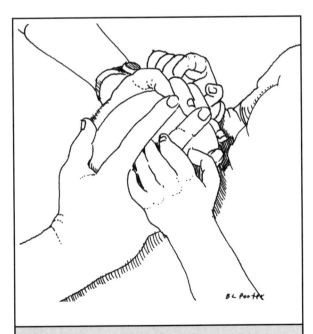

Figure 2.2   Tactile conversation: Exploring an orange

Figure 2.3   "This smells good"

- Determine the child's preferences and use those actions or objects in your interaction and in your development of conversations.

- Observe how the child responds to being touched and use those actions in your interaction and in your development of conversations. For example, if the child pats your hand, you can develop a patting game.

- Observe how the child responds to being touched and use the type of touch that is the least intrusive. For instance, put your hand beside the child's so your hands are touching and observe his or her response to determine whether you should take his or her hand.

- Provide time for the child to process information and observe the child for an anticipatory response. In general, wait longer than you might for a child of the same age who is not disabled.

- Attend to, interpret, and respond immediately to the child's communicative behaviors.

- Allow the child to respond by the most efficient means for him or her. These means could include pointing, touching a symbol, or handing over a symbol. Do not force a child to interact with you in a specific way.

COMMUNICATION DURING ACTIVITIES

Think of ways to communicate during everyday activities. For instance, keep in mind the following approaches:

- Conduct an ecological assessment to identify opportunities for interactions and tactile adaptations that are needed to engage the child's participation. An *ecological assessment* involves observing the activities that occur during the child's day, and an *ecological inventory* involves making a list of the steps or sequence of an activity. See Table 2.2 for a sample ecological inventory for circle time. In this example, the child, who is blind with multiple disabilities is also ambulatory. The sighted peer who wants to be a human guide should be encouraged to request permission of the teacher and the child who is blind.

- Communicate during these activities when it makes the most sense and does not distract the child or interfere with the activity.

- Identify situations that motivate the child's communication and in which tactile communication will be used consistently (for example, offering choices during meals or recess).

	TABLE 2.2 ECOLOGICAL INVENTORY: CIRCLE TIME		
Steps in routine	**Natural and usual instructional cues**	**Skills required**	**Tactile adaptations**
• Transition from free play to circle time	• Teacher says, "Five more minutes to play" or "Circle time" • Other children put toys away	• Follow directions • Put toys on shelves and in bins	• Tactile signs • Tactile modeling • Object cue for circle time • Tactile prompts
• Go to circle area • Sit on rug	• Adult sits at circle area • Rug	• Walk to circle area • Locate space on rug to sit down	• Peer buddy as human guide • Tactilely scan to locate free space in rug • Tactile prompts
• Sing opening song	• Teacher sings • Other children sing • Know expectation	• Know song • Sing along	• Actions, movements in time to music and signs • Tactile modeling
• Select next activity	• Teacher says, "What do you want to do next?" • Teacher provides options • Personal preference	• Listen to options • Indicate choice	• Tactile signs • Objects to represent options • Child indicates choice by giving selected object to teacher

CONTINUED ON NEXT PAGE

	TABLE 2.2 (CONTINUED)		
Steps in routine	Natural and usual instructional cues	Skills required	Tactile adaptations
• Choose center	• Teacher discusses activities • Teacher shows objects (for example, cookie cutters, computer disk, paint brush) • Personal preference	• Listen to teacher • Look at objects • Indicate choice by raising hand	• Tactile signs for activities • Duplicate objects (for example, CD) to represent centers (for example, computer center) • Indicate choice by selecting object and raising hand • Tactile prompts
• Transition to centers	• Teacher calls names and gives each child a picture that matches the selected activity • See center	• Listen for name • Recognize name • Stand up and walk to teacher • Obtain picture and go to appropriate center	• Tactile name sign • Physical prompt • Teacher gives the child with visual impairment an object and his or her peer buddy a picture that represent the same center • Peer buddy guides child to center

- Use tactile communication frequently and consistently with the child during daily meaningful and age-appropriate activities and across home, school, and community settings.

- Repeat interactions across natural opportunities. A child needs many opportunities to understand what is expected. This is true for any young child, but it is particularly true for children who do not have clear access to visual and auditory information. Identify several opportunities throughout each day that will enable the child to learn specific skills. For example, if the child is learning to make a choice between two objects that represent different activities, provide these types of choices throughout the day. Have the child make choices between foods, drinks, play activities, and clothing. Take advantage of frequent opportunities at home, school, and in the community to offer the child a choice.

needs, abilities, experiences, and daily activities. Cues and symbols must be accessible to the child, represent the child's interests and, when possible, have a close physical association to the referent (for example, a cup to indicate "drink"). Then, take the following steps:

- Use a few easily discriminated (very different) cues or symbols consistently, and gradually expand them as the child understands their meaning.

- Encourage two children to play side-by-side with different materials, and provide opportunities for the child with multiple disabilities to participate in turn-taking with objects and other ways of communicating with the other child.

- Create situations in which the child can experience other peers and adults using the same communication system for similar purposes (for example, Mary puts her hand under Sam's to use his textured symbols while she talks to Sam).

WAYS TO SUPPORT COMMUNICATION

Take the Initial Steps

Select the communication modes that will be the most efficient given the child's

Shape a Communicative Response

First, make sure that the child is positioned securely and comfortably. Then, get the child's attention through verbal and tactile contact as appropriate. Try the following methods to obtain a response:

- Offer the child an object or symbol that represents a favorite activity by placing it right next to and touching the child's hand.

- Wait for at least 10 to 15 seconds. The length of time that is necessary to wait for a child to touch, explore the object, or to make the effort to respond will vary according to the needs of an individual child. Some children need considerably longer to respond. Observe how much time it takes the child to respond to a favorite activity and to a disliked activity to obtain an estimate of the child's response time. Also, children's responses may be very subtle; for example, some children who have limited hand movements may react to touching an object by changing their muscle tone, rate of breathing, or facial expression.

- If the child does not respond, then introduce the item under the child's palm or on the child's back (or other body part) as appropriate for the individual child.

- Look for any movement from the child on the item as an indication that he or she is aware of the item.

- Use hand-under-hand guidance or a wrist prompt (that is, touch or guide the child at the wrist) to help the child explore and grasp the item.

- Immediately engage in the activity.

- Provide opportunities during the activity to feel the item and to engage in conversation about the ongoing activity and relevant items.

- Interpret the child's reactions and respond appropriately.

- Repeat the communication cycle as appropriate.

Create a Need to Communicate

The next step is to create a need to communicate. Use the following tips to encourage a child to communicate voluntarily:

- Follow the child's interests and preferences to identify key cues, symbols, and signs that the child will be motivated to learn.

- Establish predictable routines and activities to help the child understand the meaning of cues and their referents.

- Pause and wait or "interrupt" motivating activities and games to facilitate the child's expressive communication (request). For example, stop pushing the child on the swing and wait for him or her to indicate a request for more by moving his or her body, vocalizing, or signing MORE or SWING.

- Wait before beginning a very familiar and highly preferred activity. This delay strategy may elicit the child's expressive communication. For example, Figure 2.4 shows waiting for a child to sign SLIDE before going down the slide and touching the child's elbow to encourage the child's expressive communication (signing SLIDE).

- Give the child a desired item that requires him or her to ask for help (for example, a snack that he or she cannot open).

- Give the child a limited quantity of something that he or she likes to encourage a request for more.

- Offer choices on a regular basis throughout the day.

- Offer the child something that is disliked or unwanted to allow a rejection.

- Place favorite objects out of reach for the child to request.

- Violate a familiar routine or expectation to encourage the child to

"comment" (for example, place a favorite toy in the refrigerator).

Take the Next Step

Once the child seems to recognize an object cue, textured symbol, or manual sign (for example, if the child smiles or gets excited in anticipation of a favorite activity), check to see whether the child understands its meaning (for example, by

Figure 2.4 Prompting child to sign SLIDE

opening his or her mouth when presented with the sign for EAT or moving toward the location of the activity when given the object cue for art time). How does the child indicate that he or she understands the meaning of the object cue, textured symbol, or manual sign? How does he or she respond if you delay offering the anticipated activity or begin another activity instead of the anticipated one?

When the child makes the connection between object cues and their referents, gradually replace concrete object cues (for example, a spoon to represent lunch or a piece of chain for the swing to represent recess) with more abstract ones (for example, a lunch ticket to represent lunch or a textured card to represent recess) and increase the number of cues or symbols to expand the child's vocabulary. Make one change at a time; do not replace more than one object cue at a time. Increase opportunities for the child to use familiar object cues, textured symbols, or manual signs in multiple situations, with different people (including peers), and across settings. When offering choices, try to increase the numbers of options.

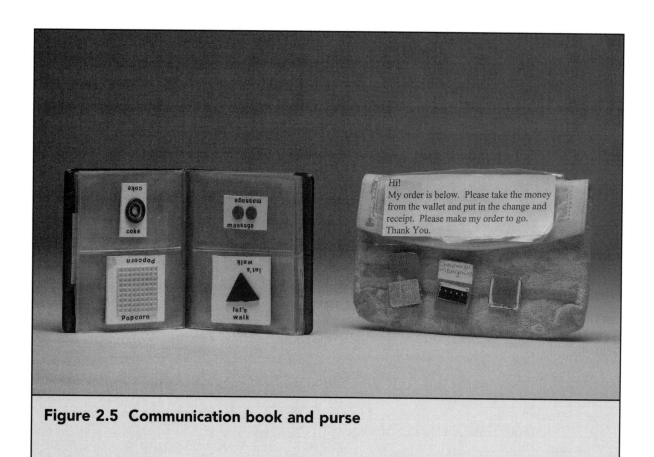

Figure 2.5 Communication book and purse

REQUIREMENTS FOR A COMMUNICATION SYSTEM

The child's educational team and family members should agree on the most effective communication modes and tactile strategies that will be used with the child. To do so, they should consider developing a picture and text dictionary of the child's communication system so that selected cues, symbols, and signs are used accurately and consistently (Mirenda, 2005). Organize these communication symbols in a display (for example, a book, board, photo album, wallet, CD holder, or communication board) that is portable and accessible to the child at all times. Figure 2.5 shows a communication book and purse. Make sure the displays take into account the child's age, interests, physical abilities, daily activities, and experiences. They should be labeled with words, phrases, or questions so communication partners can understand the message.

Service providers and family members need to document how frequently children use the selected cues, symbols, or signs and note the child's responses. Once the child has been exposed to consistent use of the communication system, determine whether the child understands the meaning of selected cues, symbols, or signs. For example, does the child understand the object cue (dog leash) for walking the dog? What does the child do if you give him a leash and wait for his or her response before leaving the house? Update the communication dictionary after regular meetings with the family or educational team to determine and document what is working, what needs to be changed, and what needs to be added.

SUMMARY

Supporting meaningful interactions with the child results in tactile conversations. Specific strategies can be employed to help the child anticipate an interaction and recognize the need to reciprocate. To effectively support tactile interactions, consider the child's unique interests and abilities. Identify specific opportunities for common interactions and then implement a systematic shaping procedure to teach the child targeted behaviors. As the child begins to demonstrate desired behaviors, the communication system can be further refined and expanded.

Chapter 3

Assessing Tactile Skills and Planning Interventions

Each child with multiple disabilities ought to receive a comprehensive assessment to determine how he or she receives information and the most effective and efficient means of supporting his or her communication. This assessment involves a careful and systematic process of gathering information. Observations on the child's use of touch and response to tactile information are important components of assessing children who have visual impairments.

Teachers and family members of children with visual impairments and multiple disabilities have many questions concerning the best way of providing tactile information and the most effective ways of teaching children to use their hands. This situation is further complicated when the child has a hearing loss as well as severe physical disabilities and cannot use his or her hands to gain tactile information. Here are some questions commonly asked by families and teachers:

- How should teachers help children to use their hands to explore and identify tactile materials?

- When guiding a child's manual exploration, should the child's hands be over the teacher's hands or under them?

- What should I do if the child prefers to use other parts of the body to explore materials?

- How are adaptations made for the child who needs tactile input but has severe physical disabilities and cannot easily control hand movements?

- How can we encourage children to use their hands when they pull them away or refuse to touch what we offer?

Answers to these questions require careful and systematic observation of the individual child, trial and error, a comprehensive analysis of the child's tactile environment, and an understanding of his or her response to and use of tactile information. (See the "Frequently Asked Questions" in Chapter 7.) In addition, teachers and family members need to determine how best to interact with the child using tactile strategies and how to represent information tactilely. Some children may resist using their hands for tactile interactions if they have had unpleasant experiences, such as having their hands manipulated or touching textures they dislike or being forced to participate in activities that they do not understand. Therefore, it is important to obtain information regarding the child's past experiences in learning to use the tactile sense.

The process of gathering information about a child's tactile experiences and use of tactile information involves comprehensive discussion with family members and relevant service providers and careful and systematic observations during typical activities and in structured situations to elicit the child's tactile exploration and interaction. This chapter contains a format for conducting family interviews and making observations about the child's use of touch and access to the tactile environment. The chapter also provides samples of discrepancy analyses and the use of prompt hierarchies for assessing the child's tactile skills and planning interventions.

GUIDELINES FOR CONDUCTING INTERVIEWS

The purpose of the family interview is to gather selected information about the child's tactile experiences in order to develop an understanding of the child's skills and needs and appropriate instructional strategies. Interviewers need to be prepared to discuss the interview questions in an efficient, nonthreatening, respectful, culturally sensitive, and family-friendly manner. This interview is more of a "conversation" with the family rather than a formal procedure. Thoughtful planning and preparation are conducive to productive and beneficial interchanges. The following are some guidelines for the three phases of interviews—preparation, the interview proper, and concluding the interview.

Getting Ready

1. Review the questionnaire and be familiar with the intent of each question so appropriate probes can be used and questions can be modified as needed to clarify comments and to maintain a conversational tone.

2. Conduct a practice interview, record the session, listen to the recording, and evaluate the process.

3. If possible, obtain feedback on the practice session from a colleague and incorporate suggestions to improve the interview process.

Conducting the Interview

1. Describe the importance and purpose of the conversation for the family and

the approximate time it will take. For example: "*You know about* _____. *We need your help to figure out*_____. *The information we get from our discussion will be used to develop tactile learning strategies for*_____. *Our discussion will take about* _____. *Let me know if you need to stop and we can schedule another time that is convenient for us to meet again.*"

2. Remind the family members that you will need to make notes. Explain confidentiality procedures and request permission to record the conversation if needed.

3. Modify the questions to fit the child and family. For example, use the child's name and refer to any previous observations you've made with the family. Omit questions that are not relevant or expand others to provide additional information that the family wants on the topic.

4. As appropriate, make positive ("*that's a good idea*"), supportive ("*you're doing a lot*"), or neutral ("*uh huh, mm*") acknowledgments of the informant's comments.

5. Be aware of your body language and nonverbal responses to unexpected or unusual comments. Remain non-judgmental and open to other points of view.

6. Be aware of your own biases and cultural values and strive to be respectful and to learn about other cultural perspectives.

Ending the Interview

1. Thank the family members for participating in the interview.

2. Reiterate how this information will be used and explain what will happen next.

Figure 3.1 shows a sample form that can be used for a family interview with basic questions that can be used to gather important and comprehensive information about a child.

Information gathered from the discussion with the family can be summarized to identify the child's use of vision and hearing if appropriate, how he or she uses objects, likes and dislikes, strengths and needs, and ways in which the child interacts and communicates. Table 3.1 shows an example of how information can be summarized from the interview with the family of Leon S.

FAMILY INTERVIEW

Child's Name _____   Age _____

Date of Interview _____   Interviewer _____

The purpose of this interview is to find out about your child's use of different senses—especially vision, hearing, and touch. We will use this information to develop instructional strategies that will support your child's interaction and learning.

1. *Vision*

The purpose of these questions is to find out about the child's visual diagnosis and the family's impression of the child's visual impairment.

- What have the physicians, ophthalmologist, and/or optometrist told you about your child's vision problem?
- What have teachers told you about your child's visual problem?

If the child has low vision:

- How does your child use his or her vision in different activities?

PROBES ABOUT USE OF VISION

- Does the child respond to light? Sunlight? A flashlight? How does he or she behave in response to the light?
- Have you noticed your child responding to persons or objects? (Ask about the size, color, distance, movement, and location of objects and people). How do you know when the child is looking at something? Does the child have a preferred visual field—does he or she seem to see things better if those things are to the right, left, above, or below his or her face?
- Have you observed if your child likes any particular color? When have you observed this? How does he or she respond to this color?

Figure 3.1 Family Interview

2. Hearing

The purpose of these questions is to find out about the child's hearing and the family's impression of how the child uses his or her hearing.

If the child has a hearing loss:

- What have the physicians and audiologist told you about your child's hearing problem?
- What have teachers told you about your child's hearing loss?

If the child has some hearing or no hearing loss:

- How does your child use hearing in different situations? What sounds does your child respond to? How loud do the sounds need to be? How close does the child need to be to hear the sound?

PROBES ABOUT USE OF HEARING

- Does the child respond to his or her name or any specific spoken words? If so, how does he or she do?
- How does your child respond? For example, does he or she smile, blink his or her eyes, start vocalizing, stop vocalizing, or move any part of the body? Does he or she turn toward the sound source?
- Does your child seem to have better hearing on one side than the other? For instance, are his or her responses better if the sound is presented on the left or right side?

3. Other Considerations

These questions provide information about the child's other learning characteristics and disabilities.

- Does your child have any other learning needs that I should know about?
- How much time does your child need to respond to you or other familiar people?

Figure 3.1 Family Interview (continued)

CONTINUED ON NEXT PAGE

4. Strong Preferences

These questions identify the child's preferences that can be used to motivate learning and to understand the child's learning style.

- What are your child's favorite people, objects, and activities? For example, some children like certain types of toys; some prefer to interact with people; some prefer rough-and-tumble play; and others like quiet activities.
- Why do you think your child likes these things?

PROBES ABOUT PREFERENCES

About each preferred person:

- Why do you think he or she likes this person? How does your child express this preference? Does your child do something different with this person that he or she doesn't do with other people?

About each preferred object:

- Why do you think he or she likes this object? What is it made of? How does it feel? Is it the texture or the material he or she likes? How big is it? What is its shape? What does your child do with this object?
- What characteristics of objects do you think your child really likes?

About each preferred activity:

- Why do you think he or she likes this activity? Which characteristics of activities do you think your child really likes?

5. Dislikes

These questions identify what the child dislikes and reveals information about the child's learning style.

- What people, objects, and activities does your child dislike?
- Why do you think he or she reacts this way?

Figure 3.1 Family Interview (continued)

PROBES ABOUT DISLIKES

About each person:

- Why do you think your child dislikes this person? How does your child express dislike?

About each object:

- Why do you think your child dislikes this object? Is it the texture? What it is made of? What is your child supposed to do with that object?

About each activity:

- Is there any activity that your child doesn't like that we haven't mentioned yet? What is it about certain activities that don't appeal to your child?

6. **Object Use**

These questions gather information on the child's use of objects and tactile information.

- How does your child handle objects and use the sense of touch in different situations and activities?
- Does your child interact with objects using his or her hands, feet, face, or body? If so, what does he or she do?
- What is your child usually doing with his or her hands? For example, does he or she shake them, put them in his or her mouth, hold onto something, or keep them by his or her side?
- Does your child use one hand or both hands to pick up and handle an object?
- What does your child usually do with objects he or she can handle independently? For example, how does he or she manipulate it?
- How do you encourage your child to handle and examine objects using touch?

Figure 3.1 Family Interview (continued)

CONTINUED ON NEXT PAGE

7. Social Interaction

These questions gather information on the child's tactile experiences during social interactions.

- How does your child interact tactilely with you, other family members, and friends? For example: Does the child like to touch people's faces or their hands? Is it common for your child to touch you or other people? When your child reaches out and touches you or other people, why do think he or she does it, and in which situations?

- How do you and other people (family, relatives, and friends) interact tactilely with your child? Which parts of your child's body do you touch or move? Why? Have you found any particular area of his or her body that your child prefers you to touch? Is there an area of the body that your child dislikes having touched? Does your child like firm touch or light touch? Show me how you might help your child.

- When you were growing up in your family, how was touch used? For example, how was touch used for affection, greetings, interactions, discipline, or redirection?

8. Communication

These questions gather information on the child's communication behaviors and opportunities.

- How does your child communicate needs, desires, refusals or dislikes, and other ideas? For example, does he or she communicate through body movements, signs, or vocalization? How does he or she do it?

- How much time does your child take to respond when you or others communicate with him or her?

- How do you communicate with him or her? For example, do you use objects or other cues? Do you use tactile signs? Do you talk to him or her? What does he or she seem to understand?

- When is your child most attentive and responsive? At what times? With what people and for what activities?

Figure 3.1 Family Interview (continued)

TABLE 3.1 FAMILY INTERVIEW INFORMATION SUMMARY

Child: <u>Leon S, age 8 years</u>   Informant: <u>Mrs. S</u>

Vision	Hearing	Other Learning Needs
• Light and shadow perception	• Moderate to severe hearing loss	• Has very low muscle tone • Has many colds • Needs to learn how to communicate and feed himself • Sleeps a lot • Takes a long time to respond
Likes	**Dislikes**	**Strengths**
• Drinking juice • Being around people • Social initiations from others • Playing familiar games with mother and sister	• Being alone • Taking long rides in cars	• Smiles when he likes someone or an activity • Responds favorably to unfamiliar people in social interactions • Enjoys simple games that involve tactile input (for example, throwing a beach ball to another person or playing pat-a-cake) • Makes choice between two objects • Sometimes reaches for nearby objects or people

CONTINUED ON NEXT PAGE

TABLE 3.1 (CONTINUED)		
Object Use	**Social Interaction**	**Communication**
• Has a weak grasp • Drinks from a sippy cup or straw independently • Will finger some objects to gather information • Explores object by touching it when provided wrist or elbow support	• Enjoys social contact from most people • Likes being around others • Smiles appropriately	• Cries when he wants attention or is upset • Vocalizes to get attention • Makes choices between two objects (for example, a vibrating toy and a carton of juice)

COLLABORATION

It is a good strategy for service providers who work with the child to collaborate among themselves and with the child's family to obtain a detailed picture of the child's tactile experiences and to develop tactile strategies to meet the child's individual needs. Family members and relevant professionals from a variety of disciplines (for example, occupational therapy, physical therapy, deaf-blindness, visual impairment, severe disabilities, and speech and language therapy) need to work together to obtain a comprehensive picture of the child. The following questions may be used to guide discussion:

1. What is the child's usual behavioral state during interactions? Is he or she quiet, alert, irritable, drowsy, or engaged in stereotypic behaviors?

2. If the child is not available for interaction because he or she is irritable, drowsy, or engaged in stereotypic behaviors, what might be done to engage the child's attention?

3. How should the child be positioned to maintain his or her attention and participation?

4. Does the child need assistive technology or adaptive equipment to support his or her participation and manual exploration?

5. What are this child's likes and dislikes related to the use of touch and tactile information?

6. How does this child use touch in different activities, situations, and social interactions?

7. How does this child interact tactilely with familiar people?

8. How do you encourage this child to use touch to examine objects and to interact socially?

9. How do you and other service providers, peers, and family members interact tactilely with this child?

10. How do you adapt visual materials or activities based on visual input (for example, looking at books, coloring, and imitation) for this child who needs tactile input?

OBSERVATION

Observations of the Child's Use of Touch

In addition to discussing the child's tactile experiences and needs with other service providers and the family, it is important to conduct systematic observations of the child's daily activities as part of the information-gathering process. Identify the context—the place, people, materials, and activity—and carefully observe the child's

hands, face, and body movements. If possible, close your eyes and use your hands to feel the child's arm and hands. Become aware of the child's skin, muscle tone, and movement.

It may also be helpful to determine how the child uses his or her hands and for what purposes. For example, Miles (2002, 2003) has emphasized that children who are deaf-blind may use their hands for three different functions: as "tools" to interact with the social and physical environment, as "sense organs" for gathering information and self-stimulation, and as a "voice" for expressive communication. As shown in Figure 3.2, it is helpful to develop a format to note how tactile information is provided, the forms of touch that the child uses, and how the child responds to tactile information.

Observations of the Tactile Environment

In addition, carefully observe the child's physical and social environment to identify opportunities that the child has to explore, handle, and manipulate objects and physically interact with others. Use the following questions to guide your assessment:

1. How and when does the child have physical contact with others (for example, at recess, playing with peers)? How does the child respond to these physical interactions?

OBSERVATIONS OF USE AND RESPONSES TO TACTILE INFORMATION

Child's name: _____   Date: _____

Age: _____   Informant: _____

Context (activity and setting): _____   Observer: _____

_____

How is tactile information provided by people who interact with the child?

_____
_____
_____

What forms of touch (social, active, or passive) does the child use?

_____
_____

How does the child respond to tactile information?

• Awareness/reflexive behaviors (for example, startle, body movements):

• Attention/alerting behaviors (for example, reaching toward object or person, smiling, frowning, quieting):

• Discrimination and recognition behaviors (for example, responds differently to familiar and unfamiliar objects/people; shows preferences for certain objects, tactile signs):

• Comprehension behaviors (for example, demonstrates understanding of tactile sign, object or touch cues):

_____
_____
_____
_____
_____
_____
_____
_____
_____
_____
_____
_____

Other observations: _____

_____
_____

Figure 3.2 Observations of Use and Responses to Tactile Information

2. How and when does the child have opportunities to explore, handle, and use materials (for example, during a lesson on the ocean, were shells examined)?

3. How is the environment organized to encourage movement and tactile exploration (for example, does the room have specific activity areas, is the floor uncluttered, are materials available or accessible to child)?

4. What supports and adaptations are needed to facilitate the child's exploration and manipulation of objects (for example, how does the assistant or peer introduce materials to the child's hand, are objects placed on a Dycem nonslip surface, raised platform, or slant board)?

ANALYSIS OF KEY ACTIVITIES

Ecological Assessments

Once the child's usual routine has been identified, observations in natural environments of usual activities conducted, and key activities that the child needs to perform selected, these activities should be observed to determine how the child is expected to participate and what types of environmental supports are present. An ecological inventory (see Chapter 2 and the following discussion for examples) of

each key activity is needed to analyze the steps of the activity—that is, what is required—so that specific skills required for each step can be more easily identified. Once these skills have been identified, then the child's participation in each step of this activity can be examined for differences between his or her actual performance and that which was expected by the teacher. These discrepancies can be analyzed via discrepancy analysis to determine the possible cause for the differences (for example, the child can't see the material, can't hold items, or doesn't understand what is expected). The reason for the discrepancy then becomes the focus of intervention. Perhaps the child needs to be shown through tactile modeling how he or she is expected to participate and what to do in each step of the activity. Perhaps adaptations to materials or the activity are needed and then the child needs to learn how to use these adaptations to participate in the activity. Remember that any adaptations that include assistive technology should be included on the child's Individualized Family Service Plan (IFSP) or Individualized Education Program (IEP).

Once the steps of the activity that has been determined to be important for the child have been identified, the specific skills required for each step can be further analyzed to determine what the child has to do to successfully complete the step. The strengths and skills of the individual child will determine what intervention procedure will be most effective. The ecological assessment in Table 3.2 describes a preschool activity that involves playing with Play-Doh. In this example, the child's hands serve as "tools" to manipulate the Play-Doh, as "eyes" to locate materials and see what others are doing, as "ears" to receive communication, and as his or her "voice" for expressive communication (Miles, 2003). The teacher will need to tailor his or her supports to promote the child's hand use for multiple functions.

After the usual sequence of steps for a selected activity is determined and the specific skills required for each step are identified, then the student who requires assistance (for example, the student who has severe and multiple impairments) should be observed in the selected activity. The purpose is to identify areas that may make the task more difficult for this child and then determine ways to bypass such difficulties and increase the child's participation and access. As shown in Table 3.3, for example, the child's performance has been noted and the discrepancy explained for step 6 of the Play-Doh activity.

An art activity involving Play-Doh is an appropriate activity for a preschooler who is deaf-blind. However, participation in the activity requires certain skills that the child may not be able to demonstrate. For example, every step in the activity requires the ability to listen to others (the teacher or peers). Because this child has a profound hearing loss, it will be difficult for him or her to develop listening skills, so instruction should focus on alternative skills. Table 3.4 shows an example for step 6 in which the child is asked to make specific shapes from the Play-Doh.

This type of ecological assessment should take place for a number of meaningful daily activities to elicit the most accurate information possible about how the child currently obtains and uses tactile information. The advantage of an ecological inventory is that the assessment occurs in typical activities and reveals what the child can do and where that child will need adaptations and support to participate more fully. The assessment is tied directly to the child's learning needs in environments identified as meaningful by significant others. As a result, the assessment leads directly to desired intervention.

Dynamic Assessment

In dynamic assessment (Snell, 2002), the assessor or another adult facilitates the child's responses to enhance the child's participation. This adult may model the desired response, physically support the child to make the task easier, provide adapted materials, or provide supportive feedback to help the child successfully engage in the activity. For example, if a child is trying to open a jar by twisting the lid, the adult may help the child loosen the lid to make it easier to open. Although the child did not remove the lid independently, such assessment does

TABLE 3.2 ECOLOGICAL ASSESSMENT OF PLAY-DOH ACTIVITY

Identified steps	Skills required for each step
1. Go to the art table	• Hear and understand teacher's direction • See the table • Move to table • Find seat and sit down
2. Choose color of Play-Doh from available pieces	• Hear and understand teacher's question: "What color do you want?" • See color options, know preference
3. Choose tools	• See options in tub, know preference • Select tools
4. Play with (roll, pound, poke) Play-Doh	• Manipulate Play-Doh with hands • Use tools
5. Talk to others	• Hearing others say something • Having something to say
6. Make something with Play-Doh	• Hear and understand teacher make requests • Get idea of what to make or see models of others
7. Roll Play-Doh into a ball and give to teacher	• Hear and understand teacher's direction: "Time to clean up" • Make ball with Play-Doh • Respond to teacher's request: "Give it to me"
8. Return tools to tub	• Locate the tub • Put tools in it
9. Go to sink and wash hands	• Hear teacher's direction: "Wash hands" • See sink and go to it • Turn on water, use soap, wash hands, rinse, turn off water, get towel, dry hands, throw paper towel away

	TABLE 3.3 DISCREPANCY ANALYSIS OF USING PLAY-DOH		
Identified steps	**Skills required for each step**	**Child's performance**	**Basis of discrepancy**
6. Make something with Play-Doh	• Hear and under-stand teacher's request • Get idea of what to make • See models	• Puts Play-Doh in mouth, spits out	• Can't hear teacher • Can't see models • Doesn't know what to do

provide considerable information about the types of supports needed for the child to be most successful. Information is obtained not only regarding what the child can do without assistance but also what kind of assistance is most helpful to a given child. Such information ties assessment procedures directly to effective intervention.

In the example of the Play-Doh activity, the assessor may try a variety of prompts to see how the child responds. These prompts may become specified conditions (accommodations) that are documented for others to more clearly understand the child's response with support. For example, if a child does not have the physical dexterity to isolate fingers and poke at the Play-Doh or hold tools, the assessor might use a tool with a Velcro band that attaches to the child's wrist and lets him or her stab at the Play-Doh. A child who does not seem to like touching the Play-Doh may prefer this adaptation. The assessor may also demonstrate how to roll or poke at the Play-Doh by tactilely modeling these movements with the child's hands over his or hers. Once this information has been provided, the assessor can stop and observe what the child does as a result of this demonstration. To be most informative for the educational team, all accommodations made for the child need to be documented so they can provide necessary support.

TABLE 3.4 DISCREPANCY ANALYSIS WITH TACTILE INTERVENTION STRATEGIES TO SUPPORT PARTICIPATION				
Identified steps	Skills required for each step	Child's performance	Basis of discrepancy	Tactile intervention
6. Make something with Play-Doh	• Hear and understand teacher's request • Get idea of what to make • See models	• Puts Play-Doh in mouth, spits out	• Can't hear teacher • Can't see models • Doesn't know what to do	• Use tactile modeling and hand-under-hand guidance to encourage different actions (for example, patting, rolling, poking, or pounding on the Play-Doh) • Provide Play-Doh models of things to make • Put model next to the child's hands to encourage exploration

Summarizing the Assessment Information

In many situations, it may not be feasible to assess the child in all activities. In most situations, it is helpful to gather the most pertinent information in the most efficient way. In this case, identify and observe the most critical activities that involve hand use, and pass this information to the educational team to analyze and compile to provide direction for other activities. For those activities that are primarily visual (for example, coloring) or auditory (for example, listening to the teacher read a story), make accommodations to provide tactile access to the child. Instead of coloring with crayons and paper, the child can "color" by rubbing crayons over textured templates or screens, paste different textures onto paper, or create designs with pipe cleaners. Instead of just listening to a story being read, the child could listen to the story with his or her hands through tactile signing and also have an opportunity to manipulate and examine some of the objects mentioned in the book or act out actions described in the story, if appropriate. If objects are also handled by another person, there will be opportunities to engage in tactile conversations with the child (that is, by touching the object together, making comments about the object, and sharing feelings or experiences).

An identified service provider (for example, a case manager or service coordinator or teacher credentialed in visual impairments) will need to review the assessment information that has been gathered and summarize it for distribution to all team members. This summary needs to be organized, clearly written, and concise and provide an overview of the child's tactile needs while also suggesting initial strategies that might benefit the child.

Completing the Analysis

Use the following questions both to help guide the analysis of activities so that the most pertinent information can be attained and to make tactile adaptions (Downing & Chen, 2003):

1. What is the purpose or objective of the activity?

2. How will tactile access to the whole activity be provided to the child?

3. What aspect of the activity is meaningful for the child who needs tactile supports?

4. Can materials be adapted to provide tactile information that is meaningful to the student?

5. What materials will convey the key concept?

6. Have I tactilely explored selected materials without looking at them?

7. How will selected materials be introduced to the child?

8. How does the child tactilely examine materials?

9. What support does the child need to handle and explore the materials?

10. What language input is needed?

Table 3.5 provides a completed example of an ecological summary that demonstrates the following steps:

1. Identify the steps in an activity.

2. List natural cues and the skills that a child needs to make use of them.

3. Identify apparent causes of discrepancies between what the child can do and what adults expect of the child in that activity.

4. Consider essential experiences that will provide the child with access to tactile information as a basis for participating in the selected activity.

5. List adaptations, strategies, and supports that will promote the child's active participation in the activity.

Service providers are encouraged to use this type of ecological inventory to develop a plan for using tactile strategies and adaptations for an individual child who requires these supports.

Based on the identified questions, the ecological inventory in Table 3.5 identifies the purpose of the activity—to read a book—and the tactile adaptations and supports that are needed to engage Stacey's participation. Because Stacey cannot see or hear or read, she needs a tactile book. She can learn to read the book by feeling and identifying tactile items, while learning the braille and tactile signs that represent key words. Procedures for reading a book should be maintained so that Stacey can understand the concept of "a book"—that is, that a book contains information and the reader needs to turn pages and progress from the first to the last page. Each book topic will determine what tactile item will be used to represent various ideas and what key words will be signed to explain what is meant by each symbol.

The adult making the materials must "read" the book tactilely to ensure that the materials used are the most tactilely salient for Stacey. So that Stacey may decide which book she prefers, they can be slowly slipped under her hands while her mother or sibling tactilely explores the book covers with her. If she does not spontaneously reach out and feel for items on each page, she can be given a gentle nudge at the elbow or be prompted to feel her caregiver's hands moving next to hers to feel the page. Given her physical skills, she'll probably need hand-under-hand support

TABLE 3.5 SAMPLE ECOLOGICAL ASSESSMENT

Child: <u>Stacey</u>   Date: <u>March 5, 2006</u>   Activity: <u>Reading a book at home</u>

Steps in activity	Natural cues and skills required to use them	Causes of discrepancies in child's performance
Get book to read	• Have books available • Want to read • Know where books are kept	• Can't see books or don't know where they are located • Limited knowledge of reading
Find place to read	• Know available options • Desire a comfortable place to sit	• Cannot see to find a free area • Can't move to area on own
Open book and read	• Have print and pictures in book • Know how to read	• Little experience with books • Cannot see print or pictures • Limited physical skills to open book
Put book away when finished	• End of book • Knows where books are to be returned based on past experience	• Limited physical skills to put book away • Doesn't know where book came from

Adaptations, strategies, and supports	Experiences that provide access to tactile information
• Parent or sibling (reading partner) offers two different tactile books for child to indicate choice by examining material on cover • Reading partner asks child to indicate preference by keeping one	• Touching other people's hands while they are getting books • Handling tactile books and turning pages; touching materials on page • Using orientation and mobility (O&M) skills to locate bookcase and get book
• Reading partner offers child a pillow or piece of material from chair to indicate whether to read in bed or on chair	• Using O&M skills to locate area to sit and by following reading partner • Sitting in different comfortable places
• Reading partner encourages child to turn book in correct orientation and to examine items on pages • Reading partner uses tactile signing and mutual tactile attention to discuss book	• "Reading" tactile book with items representing familiar family activities (for example, going on a picnic) along with print or braille for the story line • Encouraging child to touch each item on the page and feel the braille • Using tactile signs for key words
• After reading the last page, partner encourages child to close book using hand-under guidance if needed; tactilely sign FINISHED • Partner encourages child to walk (trailing or using landmarks in the room) to book shelf to put book away	• Closing book at the end and using O&M skills to take book to bookcase and put it away

to hold the book, turn pages, and actively explore each page. Careful observation of Stacey's skills across different activities following this analysis of required steps in an activity (that is, an ecological inventory) will provide considerable information about how she can actively participate and what supports she will need to do so.

FROM ASSESSMENT TO INTERVENTION

Hierarchy of Prompts

Assessment includes a consideration of the types and intensity of prompts that are required to support a child's participation in an activity or completion of a task. A prompt—an act that helps the child to initiate a response—includes verbal requests ("sit down"), gestures (pointing to a chair), modeling (sitting in a chair), and physical assistance (physically helping the child to sit in the chair). They may be used separately or combined (for example, both verbal and physical assistance). The term "hierarchy of prompts" refers to an order in the systematic use of prompts, from those that involve the most to least assistance or vice versa.

For example, to develop an understanding of what is expected and how to handle and manipulate an object, some children *may* need hand-over-hand guidance in the beginning, even after they have

observed a demonstration. However, it is most important to *fade the prompt—that is, to switch to a prompt that offers a lower level of assistance, such as providing support at the child's wrist or elbow—as soon as possible* so that the child will become more active and less passive. The effective use of prompts is a critical part of successful intervention and instruction.

Instructional Strategies

A child who is visually impaired needs to have control over his or her own hands, which serve as the child's "eyes" (a means of accessing information) as well as "tools" for interacting with people and objects. In general, the recommended practice is to use the *least* amount of prompting that is effective to teach children (Westling & Fox, 2004). It is also important to consider how nonphysical prompts can be used to elicit the child's participation; for example, in the case of a child who has some vision, the adult could hold a bottle of juice over the child's cup rather than touching the child's hand as a prompt to hold out the cup. The ultimate goal is to fade all external instructional prompting in favor of the child engaging in the desired behavior according to natural stimuli in the environment. One way to avoid physically manipulating a child to do what is expected is to provide the least amount of assistance necessary and then gradually increase the level of assistance only as needed, until the child responds as desired.

Because a child who is blind uses his or her hands to "see," it is imperative that the child's hands be treated gently and with respect. Frequent manipulation of the child's hands should be avoided when possible. Furthermore, provide sufficient time for the child to respond and interact.

In general, activities must occur within a meaningful context so that the child's learning and understanding are supported by natural cues, such as the time of day, materials used in the activity, people involved, and so on. For example, the placement of mealtime utensils and food at the table as well as being present at the table, are all natural cues that prepare the child for mealtime. Some children who are blind will search for the spoon within this familiar context; others need prompts to locate the spoon. Instead of physically manipulating a child's arm and hand to grasp a spoon, the following process can be used:

1. Tap the spoon on the table so that the child can feel the vibration (and perhaps hear the sound). Wait for a few seconds. If the child does not respond, move to step 2.

2. Bring the spoon closer so that it is barely touching the child's hand but he or she can feel where it is. Wait for a few seconds. If the child does not respond, move to step 3.

3. Push the spoon partially under the child's fingers. Wait for the child to feel the spoon and your hands on it. Wait for a few seconds. If the child does not grasp the spoon, move to step 4.

4. Push the spoon further under the child's hand, press it into his or her palm, and lift the child's wrist to encourage him or her to grasp the spoon.

This strategy demonstrates the use of the "least to most prompts" instructional strategy that begins with the least support and gradually increases the amount of support to enable the child's participation in the activity. Whether or not the amount of support or level of assistance (prompts) is increased depends on the child's response. Space out the prompts in time to allow the child to understand what is expected and to respond accordingly, as seen in the preceding example. If the child is free to remove his or her hands from the activity, he or she has less reason to resist participation.

Many children who have significant disabilities have learned to depend on prompts to participate in an activity. They may wait for a verbal direction or physical cue before initiating the expected behavior. For example, when a child is at the sink, he or she may wait for a tap on the wrist (physical prompt) before turning on the faucet. In some cases, the child may perceive the physical prompt as part of the hand-washing routine. To avoid such confusion, remember to begin with the *lowest level of prompt or the least amount of guidance* needed and then gradually decrease the amount and level of prompts, rather than providing a high level of assistance. The following two example activities—making a choice between toys and eating lunch—present a framework for identifying the types of prompts and instructional strategies that facilitate a child's participation and performance.

Example Activity I: Making a Choice between Toys

The following prerequisites should be considered for this activity:

1. Preferences for toys

2. Familiarity with the toys that are offered

3. Physical ability to interact with desired toy

4. Knowledge of where the toys are located

Table 3.6 shows examples of different types of prompts from *least to most assistance,* beginning with a "natural cue" (that is, one that occurs naturally, without instruction) and ending with "physical guidance" (that is, the most amount of assistance). Examples of visual and auditory cues are included, as these types of

prompts are helpful for children who have some vision or hearing. Service providers and family members should identify the *specific* level of prompt that a child currently needs to facilitate his or her participation and then select *one type* of prompt that will be used—if possible, one that provides less support. For example, if a child reaches for a toy when given a physical prompt (such as a touch on elbow), then a less intrusive prompt (for example, touching the toys to the child's hand to encourage the child's choice-making) should be used the next time.

Once it has been determined that the child does not clearly indicate a choice for preferred items, a systematic sequence of instruction should be implemented to help the child learn how to indicate his or her choice. It is important to identify the child's favorite and highly preferred items (toys, foods, materials) and activities as well as those that he or she dislikes. The following is a sample instruction sequence for making a choice between toys:

1. Offer the child one object that represents a favorite toy or activity. He or she will indicate a choice by picking up the object or not.

2. Offer the child a choice of two toys or activities—one preferred and one disliked. It is highly likely that the child will select the preferred item over the disliked one. A similar instructional

strategy is to offer the child the target or preferred item (for example, a toy or representation of the activity) and a "foil" (a meaningless item). When the child understands that he or she can indicate a choice by selecting an item, increase the options. Offer the child a choice of two toys or activities that are equal in preference.

To encourage a child to indicate which toy he or she wants, the examples in Table 3.7 are listed from *least to most assistance* to demonstrate a gradual increase in the level of support, if needed. Take care to select the types and numbers of prompts that support an individual child's participation. More is *not* better if a child is confused by the interaction or becomes

Type of prompt	Examples
Natural cue	Time of day Toys
Verbal cue	Ask, "Which one do you want?" (speech and tactile sign) Say, "Pick one"
Auditory cue	Tap toy or squeeze squeaky toy
Visual cue	Hold up or point to each toy
Tactile modeling	Have child feel another child's hands as that child makes a choice
Tactile prompt	Touch toy to child's hand
Physical prompt	Tap child's elbow Touch child's wrist Tap back of child's hand
Physical guidance	Guide child's hand at wrist to help him or her handle each toy

TABLE 3.6 ORDER OF PROMPTS FROM LEAST TO MOST ASSISTANCE TO TEACH CHOICE-MAKING

dependent on prompts. The overall intent is to support the child's interactions and initiation and to decrease or avoid the child's dependency on external prompts. Each time before the next prompt is provided, a specified "wait time" is given (5 to 20 seconds), depending on the child's ability and needs. Waiting for the child's response is essential to avoid over-prompting the child.

Example Activity II: Going to Lunch

The following prerequisites should be considered for this activity:

1. Familiarity with the daily routine and lunch time

2. Desire to eat lunch

3. Knowledge of where the lunch table is located

TABLE 3.7 EXAMPLES OF LEAST TO MOST ASSISTANCE

Prompt	Example
1. Verbal	"What do you want?"
2. Verbal + auditory or visual cue	"What do you want?" + tap the toy on the table (if he or she can hear it) or hold up the toy (if he or she can see it)
3. Verbal + tactile prompt	"What do you want?" + touch the toy to the child's hand
4. Verbal + tactile prompt + auditory cue or visual cue	"What do you want?" + touch the toy to the child's hand + tap toy on table (if he or she can hear it) or hold up the toy (if he or she can see it)
5. Verbal + tactile prompt + physical prompt	"What do you want?" + touch the toy to the child's hand + tap back of child's hand
6. Verbal + tactile prompt + physical guidance	"What do you want?" + touch the toy to the child's hand + guide the child by the wrist to handle each toy

4. Ability to walk independently

If a child is nonambulatory, walking to the table would not be an expectation. However, showing an understanding that it is time to eat lunch by picking up a spoon might be the expected behavior once the child is positioned at the table. Table 3.8 shows examples of different types of prompts that may be relevant to this situation. Service providers and family members should identify the *specific* level of prompt that a child currently needs to

facilitate his or her participation and then select *one type* of prompt to use to help the child go to the lunch table.

It is important to determine the type of prompt that elicits the child's response with the least assistance. For example, if the child recognizes the object cue and moves toward the lunch table, then a prompt with more assistance (for example, physically guiding the child to the table) should not be used. If the child holds the object cue, moves toward the table but is

TABLE 3.8 ORDER OF PROMPTS FROM LEAST TO MOST ASSISTANCE TO HELP CHILD MOVE TO LUNCH AREA	
Prompt	Example
Natural cue	Time of day Smell of food Sounds of other children at the lunch table Hunger
Verbal cue	"Lunch time" (Speech and tactile sign)
Auditory cue	Tap on table
Visual cue	Stand by table and gesture "come" to child
Tactile prompt	Give child an object that represents lunch
Physical prompt	Touch child's shoulder from behind and push gently forward
Physical guidance	Offer child your arm and use standard human guide technique to walk to the table

distracted before sitting down, then an auditory cue (such as tapping on the table) or verbal cue (such as saying and signing LUNCH TIME) should be provided. The following is a sample instruction sequence for beginning lunch; increase the distance between the child and the lunch table and modify the level of instructional prompts as needed to support the child's success:

1. Begin with the child next to the lunch table so he or she only has to sit in his or her chair. The table and chair also serve as natural cues when the child hears "Lunch time."

2. Increase the distance so the child has to walk a few steps to find the lunch table when he or she hears "Lunch time."

3. Increase the child's distance from the lunch table and increase the level of prompts (for example, provide an object cue as a tactile prompt), if needed.

4. Provide prompts (for example, an object cue as a tactile prompt plus a human guide) as needed at the end of the activity that occurs before lunch.

SUMMARY

Ecological inventories enable service providers to identify skills, adaptations, and supports that children need during everyday activities. Ecological inventories may be conducted for any activity and in any setting (for example, home, school, or community) in which the child participates. However, given limitations in time and energy, it is most important to focus on the child's most frequent and most challenging activities. The selection, use, and fading of prompts are essential instructional supports for engaging the child's active participation within everyday activities. These procedures may be used to organize repeated and meaningful opportunities for the child's learning and communication.

This chapter presented strategies for obtaining important information regarding how a child accesses and utilizes tactile input and described assessment that involves interviewing significant others and systematic observation of the child within natural environments. Gathering relevant information with regard to the tactile sense supports more effective interventions. Thus, this chapter demonstrates the relationship between individualized and systematic assessment and relevant and meaningful intervention. Specific strategies based on assessment data are discussed in subsequent chapters.

Chapter 4

Focusing on Tactile Strategies

This chapter describes selected tactile interaction strategies to support children with visual impairments and additional disabilities in communicating, learning, and obtaining information about the world around them. It will focus on mutual tactile attention, tactile modeling, hand-under-hand guidance, and hand-over-hand guidance. These strategies should be implemented during interactions or within a conversational context and tailored to fit the child's learning and augmentative communication needs. In addition, a recommended practice when using any tactile strategy is to speak to the child in a natural way that fits the child's abilities and age.

For the purposes of this book, *tactile strategies* are defined as planned, systematic methods of using the sense of touch to support a child's understanding of information and to promote interaction and communication. A *strategy* is a plan, approach, method, or procedure for obtaining a specific goal or result, and *tactile* means that it is related to the sense of touch. Tactile strategies, then, are ways to engage children by using interactions involving touch, including adapted communication methods. These techniques promote shared activities and benefit many children with various disabilities, particularly if the children are visually inattentive and have limited communication. Instructional practices that include tactile strategies are essential for those children who cannot see clearly enough to access visual information and cannot hear or understand speech. Such strategies should always be used with visual and auditory information, as needed, to support a child's learning and understanding. Remember to take the *child's perspective* (that is, think of what the child will experience) when providing tactile information and when using tactile strategies with a child who has a significant visual impairment.

For most family members and service providers, it is more natural to use visual or auditory strategies, rather than tactile strategies. This tendency to resort to visual or auditory means has been observed in interactions with children who are visually impaired (Barraga & Erin, 1992). It takes careful observation, much effort, and systematic practice to use tactile strategies effectively with children who have multiple disabilities. This chapter provides simulation activities to assist service providers and family members in practicing the use of selected strategies.

SELECTING SPECIFIC STRATEGIES

Family members and service providers need to collaborate on the careful selection of specific strategies (see Chapter 7), use them consistently, and then evaluate their effectiveness in supporting the child's interactions and learning. Each tactile strategy has advantages and disadvantages that should be considered in relationship to the needs and abilities of an individual child and the particular situation. A certain strategy may be most effective at one time and less effective later on. As shown in Figures 4.1 through 4.6, which illustrate washing hands, most daily activities involve more than one tactile strategy. These strategies, such as hand-over-hand and hand-under-hand guidance, physical prompts,

and tactile modeling, will be discussed in this chapter. The following questions can be used to guide the selection and use of tactile strategies:

1. Have family members, service providers, and peers contributed to the selection of tactile strategies?

2. Do the selected strategies fit the child's abilities, preferences, and needs?

3. Do the selected strategies promote positive and respectful interactions with the child?

4. Do all communication partners use the selected strategies consistently?

Figure 4.1 Tactile sign for WASH

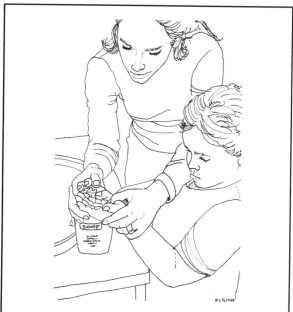

Figure 4.2 Use of hand-over-hand guidance to get soap

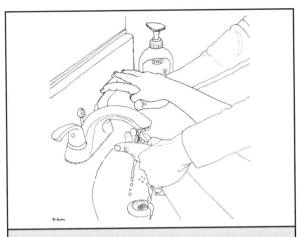

Figure 4.3 Use of hand-under-hand guidance to turn on water

Figure 4.4 Physical prompt at wrist to wash hands

MUTUAL TACTILE ATTENTION

At an early age, sighted children notice when others are looking at them, look where others are looking, and engage in joint visual attention to objects (that is, looking at an object that another person is looking at and looking at the other person). The child with significant vision loss should also have opportunities to notice when others are interested in what he or she is doing, to know what others are looking at, and to engage in joint attention through mutual tactile attention (Miles, 2002). For most people, engaging in mutual tactile attention with a child who is visually impaired

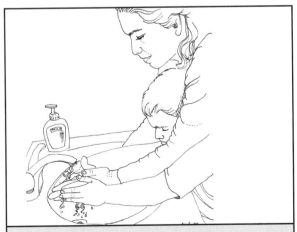

Figure 4.5 Tactile modeling to wash hands

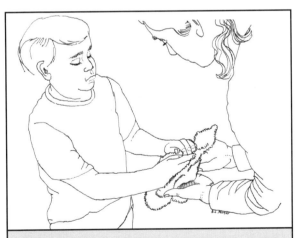

Figure 4.6 Hand-under-hand guidance to dry hands

requires careful and deliberate practice and planning. With this strategy, both the adult's or peer's hands are next to the child's hands, touching the object together and touching each other's hands, while conveying tactilely what eye contact and joint attention convey visually (looking at an object together). Mutual tactile attention involves joint attention and sharing an interaction, activity, or object through sensitive and noncontrolling mutual touch. As shown in Figure 4.7, the adult uses mutual tactile attention to follow the child's lead by focusing on what the child is doing (for example, rolling Play-Doh). In this way, it provides a means of communicative reciprocity between the child and a communication partner and encourages the child's involvement in social interaction.

Mutual tactile attention is a starting point for establishing joint attention, developing a relationship, building trust, and promoting communication. It is also helpful for children who have a severe visual impairment or those who may not understand speech or engage visually in joint attention. For example, in a first-grade class, the teacher may introduce a large seashell during a lesson about the ocean and have the children pass around and hold the shell to examine its intricacies. The child who is visually impaired touches, handles, and examines the shell and also feels that someone else is touching the shell (see Figure 4.8). In this way, the child knows that others' attention is on the shell, and the child can participate in the conversation through hand movements and tactile information. Through

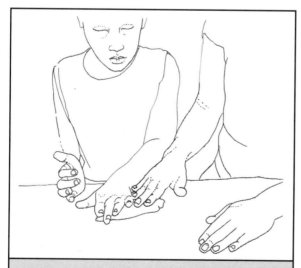

Figure 4.7 Mutual tactile attention: Rolling Play-Doh

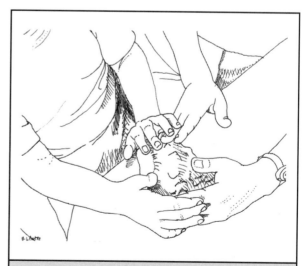

Figure 4.8 Mutual tactile attention: Examining a seashell

mutual tactile attention, the conversation might be: "This is a very interesting shell." "Yes, it is. I really like the hard points over here. Do you?"

Attending to the child's actions while using mutual tactile attention provides the conversation partner with the opportunity to carefully observe and to respond to the communicative behaviors of the child who has multiple disabilities. Mutual tactile interaction may serve a variety of communicative functions, such as requests or comments. Initially the child may not understand why another person is joining his or her activity; he or she may even reject any attempts of another person to establish mutual tactile attention. The conversation partner should join the child's activity in a gentle, quiet, and respectful way and convey his or her interest through touch and words. Repeated opportunities to engage in mutual tactile experiences along with appropriate nonverbal and symbolic communication input will support the child's understanding of the shared experiences and the messages that may be communicated. Table 4.1 illustrates the use of mutual tactile interaction and which communicative function it fulfills.

Suggestions for Practice

Mutual tactile attention enables a communication partner to demonstrate interest in what the child is doing in a way that the child can perceive—for instance, the child

> *"Each of these initial comments using touch can lead into a tactile conversation if the partner pauses, notices the child's next touch or movement, then responds or comments again with his or her own touch. Tactile conversations, involving mutual tactile attention, can become enjoyable and natural if they are practiced with care and attention to the interests of the individual child."*
>
> —B. Miles

who is blind can then understand that someone is looking at what he or she is doing. It can be used to expand the child's level of participation in an activity by including additional actions or objects. For example, the child who is exploring a shell by tapping the edges may begin rubbing the shell with his or her fingers when he or she imitates the communication partner's hand movements. At first, the communication partner imitates the child's patting the shell. Gradually, the partner begins to rub the edges of the shell with his or her fingers, thus showing the child another way to examine the shell.

Service providers need to discuss the purpose of mutual tactile attention and its potential benefit for the child who is blind with additional disabilities. Some family members and other communication partners may be reluctant to engage in mutual

TABLE 4.1 MUTUAL TACTILE INTERACTIONS AND THEIR FUNCTIONS	
Interaction	**Function**
One-year-old Tommy is playing with his hands. His mother gently puts her fingers on the back of his hand and imitates with her touch the rhythm of his touch, which communicates, "I see you playing with your hands."	Comment
Two-year-old Juan is pulling bells on a mobile. His sister touches his fingers and the bell, which communicates, "Let's play together." They take turns pulling the bells.	Invitation or request
Three-year-old Joanna is splashing in her bath. Her father puts his fingers under her hands and lightly splashes with her, which communicates, "We're splashing, that's fun!"	Comment
Five-year-old Derek is banging a drum. A friend places his hands right beside Derek's so they are touching and bangs the drum, which communicates, "That looks like fun, can I do it too?"	Request for permission
Seven-year-old Alexis is feeling the vibration of the dishwasher. Her mother puts her hand right beside Alexis's so they are touching, which communicates, "The dishwasher is on."	Comment
Ten-year-old Francisco is handling a large papier-mâché mask. His teacher puts two fingers slightly under Francisco's hand and feels the mask, which communicates, "Wow, can I see the mask too?"	Request for permission
Twelve-year-old Mai Ling is patting her dog. Her brother places his hand right beside hers and pats the dog, which communicates, "Archie's a good dog."	Comment

tactile attention with a child who is blind; they may hesitate to touch a child's hands for fear of interrupting the child's play or upsetting the child. Some communication partners may feel inhibited about touching another's hands or other parts of a child's body to obtain mutual tactile attention. Take care that mutual touch is respectful and conveys a message of interest in what the child is doing. Mutual tactile attention should be established sensitively to avoid startling or confusing the child or interrupting his or her focus on the activity.

Getting Started

Currently, mutual tactile attention is not a commonly used strategy, perhaps because it requires a different approach to interacting with children who have significant and multiple disabilities. It requires the conversation partner to carefully observe and gently join the child in what he or she is doing; that is, to follow the child's lead. In general, adults tend to use hand-over-hand or physical assistance to prompt a child who has multiple disabilities to do what the adult wants the child to do. Mutual tactile attention needs to be used more frequently and more consistently with children who are blind and have additional disabilities to evaluate its effectiveness in supporting the child's social interaction.

What follows are ways to initiate mutual touch and make it a positive experience:

- Begin by carefully observing the child's actions and behaviors to identify opportunities to engage the child in mutual tactile attention. Look at what the child does with his or her hands and the objects that he or she handles. For example, if the child pats a drum, perhaps you could join in this action.

- Decide how to place your hands close to the child's without interrupting his or her actions or movements. From your knowledge of the child, estimate whether he or she will accept your hand or fingers beside his or her hand and continue the activity—for example, to keep the child patting the drum when you do the same.

- Use the type of touch that the child prefers and is the least intrusive. For instance, if the child likes to play a piano and accepts another's fingers partially on his or her own, then when he is playing the piano, imitate his or her finger movements by placing your hand so your fingers are touching his or her hand on the keys (see Figure 4.9). The intent of this communication is, "I hear you playing the piano; I like it."

- Touch an object that the child likes and is handling. Slide a finger next to the child's fingers or under the child's fingers as if to say, "I see what you're doing. Can I join you?"

- If the child stops interacting with the object when you touch his or her hand then he or she may be communicating, "I don't want to play with you." Respect the child's communication and remove your hand as if to say, "OK, maybe we can play later."

- Once the child has accepted your interaction and you are both engaged in the activity, introduce slight changes. For example, if you are both playing with Play-Doh and poking your fingers in it, start making "a snake" by rolling it out with your hand right beside the child's hand so they are touching. However, do not force the child to do as you do.

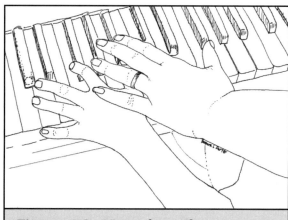

Figure 4.9 Mutual tactile attention: Playing the piano

- Notice the child's reactions and be responsive to the child's signals of hesitancy, refusal, or dislike. As with the selection and use of touch cues, many factors (for example, age, physical and cognitive abilities, family culture, and experience) will influence a child's reaction to attempts to engage him or her in mutual tactile attention.

- Always remember to be persistent and gentle. Make sure the child can feel that you are touching the object or materials with him or her. Begin by following the child's interest (movements or actions) before expanding the tactile conversation by introducing new actions or objects, and adjust your pace to the child's attention and state. Opportunities to experience the child's perspective are helpful for sighted service providers, family members, and peers in learning to interact through touch with a child who has a visual impairment. For more information about how to experience mutual tactile attention, refer to Simulation Activity 1 under "Simulation Activities" at the end of this chapter.

TACTILE MODELING

Sighted children learn by watching other people, but a child without functional vision needs frequent opportunities to feel another's actions by touching the parts of the body or objects involved in the actions. *Tactile modeling* involves demonstrating and teaching a child an action or activity through touch. In this way, a child feels (rather than sees) what another person does, so he or she is learning from a tactile model. Because the hands can only feel a small portion of an object or activity at one time, the child will need plenty of time to perceive the various aspects of the model and to integrate them into an understanding of the particular object, action, or concept. The child needs repeated access to the model over time in order to understand the actions or movements and to be able to imitate them. For example, a child may place both hands on his or her parent's or other caregiver's hands while that person

makes a sandwich. This task requires several steps—placing the bread on the cutting board, spreading jelly on one slice and peanut butter on the other, putting the slices together, and cutting the sandwich in half—so the child can only perceive a limited piece of the tactile model at any one point. Repeated opportunities to access tactile modeling of this activity is essential if the child is to understand how to make a peanut butter and jelly sandwich. Figure 4.10 shows tactile modeling for teaching the child how to open a jar, and Figure 4.11 demonstrates the use of tactile modeling for teaching the child how to spread peanut butter on bread.

Tactile modeling involves the demonstration of an activity by having the child (observer) feel the demonstrator's actions

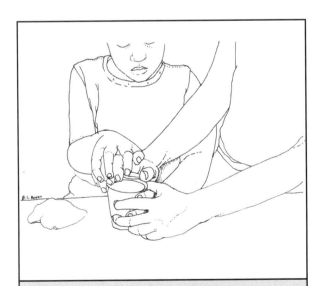

Figure 4.10 Tactile modeling: Opening a jar

Figure 4.11 Tactile modeling: Spreading peanut butter on bread

by touching parts of the body or objects involved in the action. It provides a means for a child who is blind to observe the actions of another person—a tactile means of demonstrating something to a child who is totally blind and cannot hear or understand spoken directions. It conveys information about an activity or action to a child who has severe visual impairments in a way that the child can perceive it tactilely and imitate it, if appropriate.

Tactile modeling also promotes conversational turn-taking. The communication partner demonstrates something, the child repeats it, and the communication partner provides feedback. This turn-taking may include comments and nonverbal exchanges.

The following are some examples of the use of tactile modeling:

- Linda has her 2-year-old son David sitting on her lap with his back against her. Linda sings and claps her hands between David's hands; then she stops and pauses for a few seconds. She resumes singing and prompts David to clap by tapping his hands and saying, "You clap."

- The teacher shows 5-year-old Joseph the materials for an art activity: cardboard, pieces of wood, and the glue bottle. She wants Joseph to make a collage. She puts her hands under Joseph's hands so

"In order for tactile modeling to be successful, a child needs to feel comfortable 'following' another's hands. This 'following' is learned through many gentle tactile conversations, through positive experiences of mutual tactile attention, and through repeated and respectful invitations to follow another's hands."

—B. Miles

he can feel her grasp a piece of wood, squeeze the bottle of glue, put glue on the wood, and stick it on the cardboard. She says, "Your turn," and touches the bottle of glue to Joseph's hand. If there is a sample of a desired product, then Joseph should be encouraged to feel it first.

- John swings a bat at a ball resting on a baseball tee so his friend Jeremy can feel his body position, arm movement, and grip on the bat as he hits the ball. Jeremy has previously had the opportunity to tactilely explore the bat, batting tee, and ball.

As with other tactile strategies, some children and communication partners may be uncomfortable with tactile modeling because of differences in their age, gender, relationship, culture, and experiences. Such concerns should be discussed, and family members and service providers should agree how strategies may be used and modified, if needed, to provide the child who is blind with the much-needed access to tactile information. There are limitations to the use of tactile modeling as an instructional strategy. Not all aspects of an activity can be perceived easily, completely, or safely through tactile modeling. For example, to perceive the demonstration of blowing out a candle, a child who is blind may feel the demonstrator's cheeks, lips, and breath but cannot "feel" the lit candle directly; however, he or she may handle the unlit candle. Only one aspect of an activity at a time can be perceived through tactile modeling (for example, the individual steps in making a sandwich), so for multi-step activities the child must remember a sequence of actions through tactile models. Moreover, learning from tactile modeling requires a child to have some degree of hand use and cognitive skills and the ability to synthesize information perceived tactilely. To expand on Simulation Activity 1 and to practice tactile modeling, see Simulation Activity 2: Tactile Modeling at the end of this chapter.

Suggestions for Practice

There are several ways to effectively practice tactile modeling. Set up an activity in which you and the child have the same materials, such as Play-Doh and cookie cutters. Sit beside the child and make your hands available for the child to touch them and follow their movements. Take a turn imitating the child's action on the materials (for example, poking or rolling the Play-Doh). Identify the actions or activities that can be taught through tactile modeling, such as washing hands or playing with Play-Doh. You can also allow the child to feel your hands in a variety of routine activities—during meals, playing with toys, washing hands, and so on.

Decide how best to provide a tactile model. For example, observe where and when the child wants to place his or her hands on the model to feel the actions. Model the action multiple times before expecting the child to imitate it, and provide sufficient wait time between tactile models so that the child will understand when the action is completed. For example, roll the Play-Doh back and forth with the child's hands partially over yours, stop and feel the Play-Doh, and repeat the sequence.

Observe the child's responses to the tactile model. Does the child keep his or her hand on yours? Does the child initiate the action that you demonstrated? Determine whether tactile modeling is an efficient method of instruction for an individual child given his or her individual preferences, needs, and abilities. If a child who is blind has difficulty (because of physical or behavioral limitations) keeping his or her hands on yours while you are demonstrating the action, then tactile modeling is not the most efficient strategy at this time. If the child has sufficient vision to see a demonstration, then the use of tactile modeling is time-consuming and unnecessary.

HAND-UNDER-HAND GUIDANCE

The purpose of hand-under-hand guidance is to provide gentle and supportive physical assistance to children with significant disabilities. In recent years, hand-under-hand guidance has received much attention in the field of visual impairments and deaf-blindness (Alsop, 2002; Chen, 1995; McLinden & McCall, 2002; Miles, 2002). When children require physical assistance to participate in activities or to handle objects or materials, there is a tendency to use hand-over-hand guidance and to manipulate the child's hand rather than using a less intrusive strategy. Special effort is needed to become more comfortable and proficient in using hand-under-hand guidance with children who have multiple disabilities. Guiding a child's hand by providing support *underneath* his or her hand or wrist allows the child to retain control while being in contact with a partner's hand. In this position, another person places his or her hand slightly under a child's to examine objects or to interact tactilely (Dote-Kwan & Chen, 1999; MacFarland, 1995; Miles, 2003). Because the child's hand is on top of the other person's hand (see Figure 4.12), the child knows that the other person will touch whatever is being explored first and the child is free to move his or her hand at will.

Suggestions for Practice

Hand-under-hand guidance is a useful strategy for tactile modeling (that is, to demonstrate an action to a child who is blind or visually impaired). It also encourages participation by children who are hesitant about handling particular or unfamiliar objects and who dislike being forced to do so. As shown in Figure 4.13, another person grasps the object in question (in this case, a brush) and places the back of his or her hand under the child's

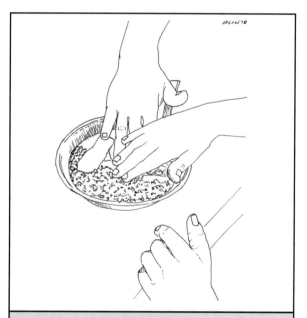

Figure 4.12 Hand-under-hand guidance: Examining materials

palm. In Figure 4.14 the person holding the object slowly rotates his or her hand so that the child will gradually come into contact with the object (see Figure 4.15). This method allows the child to control whether he or she wants to touch or handle the object. The child is free to hesitate or pull his or her hands away if uncertain about touching something (see Figure 4.16).

As an alternative strategy (shown in Figures 4.17, 4.18, and 4.19), a child can be encouraged to place his or her hand on top of another's hand while examining a surface (in this case, a page of braille). The person who is touching the surface gradually withdraws his or her hand until the child's fingers touch the surface (Dote-Kwan & Chen, 1999).

The child must have the physical ability and willingness to put his or her hand on top of another's to benefit from hand-under-hand guidance. A child with a motor problem may keep his or her hand on an adult's hand with the gentle support

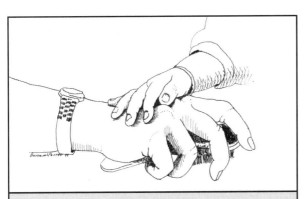

Figure 4.13 Hand-under-hand introduction of brush

Figure 4.14 Rotate hand gradually to introduce object

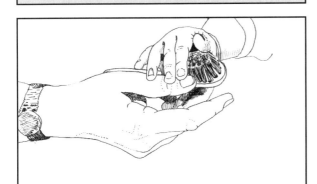

Figure 4.15 Child feels object in adult's hand

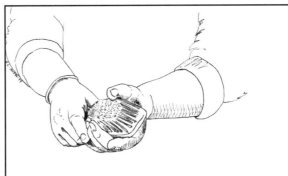

Figure 4.16 Child explores brush

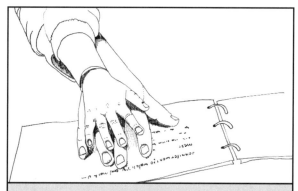

Figure 4.17 Child's hand on top of adult's reading braille

Figure 4.18 Adult gradually pulls hand back

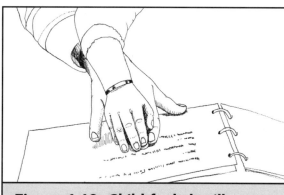

Figure 4.19 Child feels braille

of the adult's thumb or other hand over the child's hand. The use of hand-under-hand guidance should be tailored to fit each child's physical and motivational needs.

Hand-under-hand guidance is a means of helping the child make tactile comparisons during everyday activities—to feel that the bowl is empty before putting cereal in it, to notice that he has a sandal on one foot while the other foot is bare, or to feel the difference between his or her short, straight hair and a sister's long, curly ponytail. These situations are natural opportunities for tactile conversations, and the child's discovery of differences through touch provides a basis for understanding certain concepts and the meaning of related words. The child should be familiar with the person with whom he or she is using hand-under-hand guidance and be comfortable interacting with that person. The conversation partner should develop a relationship with the child by engaging in predictable activities, hand games, and other enjoyable interactions.

Consider the following questions to guide you in the use of hand-under-hand guidance:

1. In what situations will hand-under-hand guidance be an effective way to provide a child with access to people and objects in the environment? For example, hand-under-hand guidance

"When I understood the difference between the way a person who is deaf-blind uses his or her hands and the way that sighted people use their hands, I became much more careful when interacting with the hands of a deaf-blind person. People who can see use their hands mainly as tools, to interact with their environment—to pick up things, perform tasks. I think that 'hand-over-hand' techniques generally evolved from thinking about hands as tools, and from the desire to help the person perform tasks. For the person who is deaf-blind, however, his or her hands must not only act as tools; the hands must also become sense organs—they must act as eyes and ears—and must often be a voice as well. As such, they need to become very sensitive in order to get information, and very expressive in order to express ideas and feelings. I have found over the years that the best way to help a person who is deaf-blind develop these refined hand skills is to leave the hands free whenever possible. Hand-under-hand invitations to touch things and to explore allow the person who is deaf-blind to remain in control of his or her hands and to learn to use them skillfully."

—B. Miles

may help the child explore a novel or disliked object or introduce him or her to an unfamiliar person.

2. How does the child respond? Does the child know the person who is offering his or her hand? Does the child cooperate by putting his or her hand on top of the person's hand?

3. Will the child keep his or her hand on top of another person's hand long enough to access what is being shown? If not, how can he or she be encouraged to do so? Sometimes a gentle touch on top of the child's hand will keep it in place or using a finger to grasp the child's finger will maintain the hand-under-hand support.

The following are additional points to remember when providing hand-under-hand guidance:

• Be patient when encouraging a child to follow your hands. Spend time just resting your hands gently under a child's hands, letting him or her know that you are listening, that your hands are trustworthy. Gradually, the child can learn to follow your hands to get information about the world (Miles, 2003).

• Encourage early use of hand-under-hand guidance with a young child so he or she will become comfortable and familiar with this strategy.

- Help the child who has a motor problem keep his or her hand on yours by gently rolling one of your fingers over his or hers or by gently placing a finger of your other hand on the back of the child's hand.

Simulation Activity 3, at the end of this chapter, offers a specific way to practice hand-under-hand guidance.

HAND-OVER-HAND GUIDANCE

Hand-over-hand guidance is extremely common, but it is perhaps the most intrusive prompting strategy. It occurs when someone takes the child's hands to make him or her do something. This strategy is frequently used to help children explore objects, act on objects, perform tasks, or produce manual signs (Freeman, 1985;

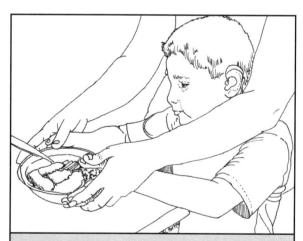

Figure 4.20 Hand-over-hand guidance: Carrying a bowl

McInnes & Treffry, 1982), particularly those children who are unresponsive or unfamiliar with the activity. For an example, see Figure 4.20, which demonstrates carrying a bowl using hand-over-hand guidance. This technique should be used gently, respectfully, and cautiously, given that the child may not be actively participating and has little control over the process. Further, the person using this technique must have a trusting relationship with the child and needs to be very attentive and responsive to the child's reactions.

One disadvantage to the use of hand-over-hand guidance is that the child may be more attentive to the person's hand over his or hers than to the movement, action, or activity that is being demonstrated. Another problem is that the person who is physically guiding the child's hand determines when, how, and where the child moves his or her hand and what he or she touches. Over time, this lack of control may result in reluctance and then resistance of some children to having their hands manipulated. Imagine having someone—particularly if he or she is unfamiliar—take your hand and force you to touch something slimy or very sharp without any visual preparation or understanding of what is about to happen. The typical response in such a situation would be to resist and pull one's hand away. Other children may become prompt-dependent and wait for another's hand on theirs as a prompt to initiate an action (Downing,

2003; Miles, 2003). See Simulation Activity 4 for a way to experience hand-over-hand guidance.

The hands of a child with little or no vision are similar in function to the eyes of a child with vision—a significant means of gaining information. As such, the child's hands should not be manipulated without careful and respectful consideration. In some situations, a child may seem to request hand-over-hand guidance; then you may gently help him or her, for example, when teaching a child a simple action such as combing his or her hair. The following are some points to remember when using hand-over-hand guidance:

- Use it sparingly.

- Be aware of the child's reactions and respond accordingly.

- Fade the use of hand-over-hand as soon as possible to a less intrusive prompt (for example, touching or supporting at the wrist).

Hand-over-hand guidance may be effective with a child who has very limited hand use and needs gentle assistance to handle objects. However, this strategy should be used only when necessary and with careful observation and sensitivity to the particular child's reactions. The degree of assistance should be decreased as appropriate to increase the child's active participation. See Figure 4.21, which demonstrates a decrease in physical assistance to help the child read a braille book. Less intrusive strategies should be considered and used whenever feasible. Consider the following questions in your use of hand-over-hand guidance:

1. Am I aware of when the child is using his or her hands to explore and when he or she is manipulating objects?

2. Am I careful not to interfere with the child's exploration?

3. What strategies other than hand-over-hand have been used to support this

Figure 4.21 Hand-over-hand guidance: Reading a braille book

child's participation? If so, how does he or she respond to them?

4. Am I aware of when the child "requests help" in manipulating objects?

5. How am I guiding the child's hands with mine?

6. How does the child respond?

7. How will I reduce the amount of support provided by hand-over-hand guidance? (See Chapter 3 for a discussion of ways to reduce the level of assistance in physical prompts.)

SIMULATION ACTIVITIES

Simulation Activity 1: Mutual Tactile Attention

1. Pair up with another person. Take turns playing the role of the child who is visually impaired and the sighted communication partner.

2. The "child" closes his or her eyes and engages in exploration or use of an object (for example, patting a drum or tapping and poking at Play-Doh).

3. Without speaking or signing, the sighted partner uses *mutual tactile attention* to interact with the child by focusing solely on the child, placing his or her hand so it touches the child's and imitating the child's actions.

4. After both people have had a turn being the child and the communication partner, discuss the experience. How did this feel? What did you discover?

Simulation Activity 2: Tactile Modeling

1. Begin by taking turns playing the role of the child who is visually impaired and the sighted communication partner. The "child" closes his or her eyes and engages in exploration or use of the object (for example, patting a drum or tapping and poking at Play-Doh).

2. Without speaking or signing, the sighted partner uses *mutual tactile attention* to interact with the child by focusing solely on the child, placing his or her hand so it touches the child's and imitating the child's actions.

3. The sighted communication partner *gradually* introduces another action with the object (for example, rolling the Play-Doh, changing the rhythm of the pats on the drum) through tactile modeling by gently using hand-under-hand guidance.

4. After both people have had a turn being the child and the communication partner, discuss the experience. How did this feel? What did you discover?

Simulation Activity 3: Hand-under-Hand Guidance

1. Begin by taking turns being the child who is visually impaired with additional disabilities and the sighted communication partner. The "child" closes his or her eyes and sits quietly.

2. Without speaking or signing, the sighted partner uses social touch to greet the "child" and then shows him or her a new toy, how to play with it, or how to manipulate an object using *hand-under-hand* guidance. Try different ways of keeping in contact with the child's small hand; if it tends to move or slip off your own hand, for example, use your finger to grasp one of the child's fingers that is on top of yours, or gently place a finger of your other hand on top of the child's hand.

3. After both people have had a turn playing the role of the "child" and the communication partner, discuss the experience. How did this feel? What did you discover? Any challenges?

Simulation Activity 4: Hand-over-Hand Guidance

1. Begin by taking turns being the child who is visually impaired with additional disabilities and the sighted communication partner. The "child" closes his or her eyes and sits quietly.

2. Without speaking or signing, the sighted partner uses social touch to greet child and then shows him or her a new toy, how to play with it, or how to manipulate an object using *hand-over-hand guidance*. Try different ways of guiding the child's hand with yours; for example, guide with your hand on top of the child's hand and then at the child's wrist. Try introducing items that are unexpected or unpleasant to touch (for example, a blob of hair gel, a thumb tack, or steel wool).

3. After both people have had a turn being the "child" and the communication partner, discuss the experience compared with using the *hand-under-hand* technique. How did this feel? What did you discover? Were some items unpleasant to handle? Was it difficult to encourage the "child" to handle certain items?

SUMMARY

Tactile interaction strategies are systematic efforts to help the child understand information through the sense of touch. Obviously critical for the child unable to benefit from visual or auditory input, such strategies also have implications for children with other types of severe and multiple disabilities. Several strategies were described in this chapter with suggestions as to when and how to apply them. Recognizing the difference between using tactile strategies and being the recipient of such strategies is an important consideration. Service providers are encouraged to become aware of how they intervene through the sense of touch and to try to understand the child's perspective as the recipient of the interaction. Each child is unique, and therefore, tactile strategies must be individually determined to be most effective.

Chapter 5

Considering Multiple Communication Options

Communication creates a sense of belonging to a family, group, and community. Imagine what it must be like to be unable to communicate with another person—to be unable to make your needs, wants, and ideas understood. Imagine the feelings of frustration, helplessness, and isolation a person feels if he or she does not have an effective way to convey or understand a message. A mutually understood means of communication is the key not only to social relationships but also to learning. A child must have a means of communication to understand what is being taught (receptive communication) and to demonstrate knowledge (expressive communication).

Communication involves sharing a message between at least two people. *Receptive communication* is the understanding of that message, and *expressive communication* is the creation and sharing of that message with another. Messages can be expressed in many different forms (Beukelman & Mirenda, 1998; Downing, 2005a)—through facial expressions, body language, speech, manual signs, print,

gestures, and pictures. Some forms of communication are very abstract—speech, written messages, and manual signs; other forms are less abstract—gestures, facial expressions, objects, and pictures—and may be easier to understand. There are many forms of communication that may be used receptively and expressively. When children have sensory, cognitive, or other disabilities, instruction in appropriate communication modes—depending on their individual needs—that can be used without vision, hearing, or symbolic skills is essential for their development and overall well-being. A child with multiple disabilities may need a variety of communication forms, different ways to receive a message, and other ways to express messages efficiently, and may need to use a variety of modes depending on the situation and communication partner. For example, a child who is blind and has a mild hearing loss and other disabilities may be able to discriminate and recognize spoken words but will rely on manual signs and objects for expressive communication. In addition, this child may sign key words to communicate with partners who know sign language and use objects with those who do not.

This chapter describes a range and variety of communication options that may be used with children who have visual impairments and multiple disabilities. First, it provides an overview of communication symbols—from concrete to abstract and including visual symbols—and next, it focuses on selected tactile communication options.

COMMUNICATION SYMBOLS

There are many different types of symbols to support the communication and language skills of individuals who do not use speech. The fields of linguistics and alternative and augmentative communication have identified the relationship between a symbol and what it represents as being both *arbitrary* and *entirely learned* (Fuller, Lloyd & Schlosser, 1992; Venkatagiri, 2002). In the United States, some authors in the field of deaf-blindness have used the term *symbol* to mean a representation and the term *tangible symbols* to mean a communication system that includes three-dimensional symbols (objects) and two-dimensional symbols (photographs and drawings) for children who do not understand the meaning of abstract symbols (Rowland, Schweigert & Prickett, 1995; Rowland & Schweigert, 2000). The purpose of tangible symbols is to provide a receptive and expressive means of communication that allows reference to people, objects, places, concepts, and events beyond the immediate context and that fits the child's sensory and cognitive abilities and experiences. Tangible symbols are not standardized and are usually developed for an individual child. However, the Texas School for the Blind has developed standard tactile symbols that they use with their students who are blind and have additional disabilities, including those who are deaf-blind. This extensive list includes symbols for the categories of time, events, places, people, emotions, objects, food, actions, miscellaneous function words, and gym symbols (Hagood, n.d.).

Developing an individualized alternative communication system requires the consideration of a range of symbols, from abstract to concrete (Mirenda, 2005). Children may use certain types of these symbols for expressive communication and different ones for receptive communication, but most children with multiple disabilities will probably use a combination of these symbols depending on their abilities, needs, motivation, and the demands of the communicative setting. Although the following list is not intended to impose a strict continuum from abstract to concrete symbols, its purpose is to facilitate the selection and development of the most efficient communication systems for individual students.

Traditional Orthography or Braille

Traditional orthography, including print for those who see and *braille* for those who don't have functional vision, is a standardized and abstract symbol system consisting of letters formed by a unique visual (lines) or tactile (raised dots) character. Stringing a series of these characters together creates words, which in turn stand for specific referents. The string of characters, whether visual or tactile, does not resemble its referent and is considered abstract in its representation. For example, the written word "cup" in either print or braille has no visual relationship to its meaning (see Figure 5.1).

Textured Symbols

Textured symbols are individually created for students who need a tactile and static system. Given textures, such as cotton, leather, plastic, or dried glue dots, are affixed to cards and used by the student to indicate desired and specific items, people, or activities. The majority of textured symbols will have no relationship to what they represent and are therefore considered to be an abstract communication system. For example, a pattern of glue dots might represent "going for a swim" (see Figure 5.2). Occasionally, an effort is made to have the texture have some relationship to what it is intended to represent. For example, a small piece of tile means a desire to go to the bathroom, which has tiles on the walls.

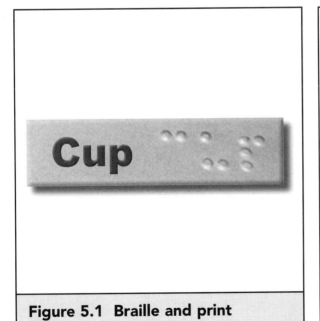

Figure 5.1 Braille and print

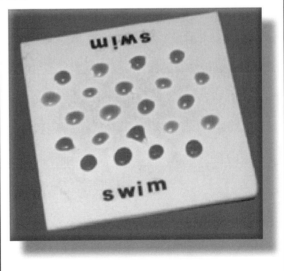

Figure 5.2 Textured symbol

When texture symbols closely resemble what they represent, they are less abstract and more iconic. The close relationship between an iconic textured symbol and what it represents may help some students to more easily understand its meaning compared to a more abstract textured symbol.

Manual Signs

Manual signs can be a visual or tactile means of communication using vocabulary from American Sign Language (ASL). Each sign—made with one or two hands and with a specific hand shape, orientation, placement on the body or articulation in space, and movement—represents a word or words that convey meaning. ASL is a visually and spatially based language with a distinct structure and syntax (Fisher & Siple, 1990; Kilma & Bellugi, 1979). Although signs are usually presented visually at a distance from the receiver, when used tactilely, the signer produces signs under the hand of the communication partner who does not see or hear. The receiver tactilely recognizes the signs because of their characteristics—hand shape, location, orientation, and movement. The majority of signs in ASL—for example, MOTHER (see Figure 5.3)—do not resemble their referent and are considered abstract. However, several signs—for example, BABY, DRINK, CUP, and LOOK—look similar to their referent and are considered to be more iconic. Other signs—for example, DOG, TREE, CAT, FISH, and SPIDER—bear a relationship to one or more aspects of their referents and are considered to have greater iconicity than completely abstract signs such as HATE, LIKE, and HAPPY. The more iconic signs may be easier for children with multiple disabilities to learn. For expressive communication purposes, the child must have adequate physical dexterity to form the manual signs needed for this system. Modified signs that meet the cognitive and physical needs of the user may be easier to learn and use but harder for others to perceive and understand.

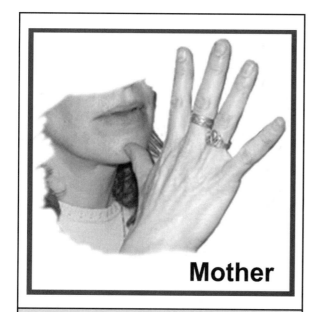

Mother

Figure 5.3 Sign MOTHER

Blissymbols

Blissymbols, developed by Charles Bliss, contain primarily abstract visual symbols that serve as an alternative to traditional orthography (Blissymbolics Communication Institute, 1984). Based on a logical system that allows the user to create any message, visual markers are added to symbols to change syntax and pragmatic functions. Whereas many Blissymbols are quite abstract, several are iconic and therefore easier to understand (Mizuko, 1987). For example, the shape of a heart can represent the noun "heart." When an arrow pointing up is placed next to the heart shape, the word conveyed is "happy." If the arrow points down, the word becomes "sad." The Blisssymbols for money, time, and animal resemble an aspect of their referent (see Figure 5.4). While primarily visual, Blissymbols also can be designed to be tactile.

The logical nature of the system plus its visual iconicity are believed to help students learn the meanings of the symbols.

Lexigrams and Logos

Lexigrams and logos are primarily visual symbols but can be designed to be three-dimensional and, therefore, tactilely perceived. Lexigrams or logos are shapes, with or without color, that represent different referents. Although considered abstract, many of these shapes can closely resemble referents—for example, the universal logos for male and female restrooms resemble the silhouette of a man or woman. The logo indicating access or parking for individuals with disabilities (see Figure 5.5)

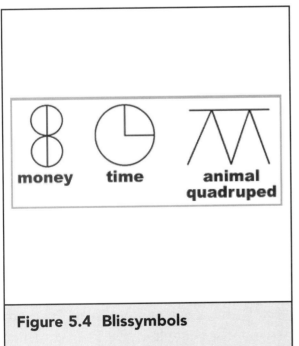

Figure 5.4 Blissymbols

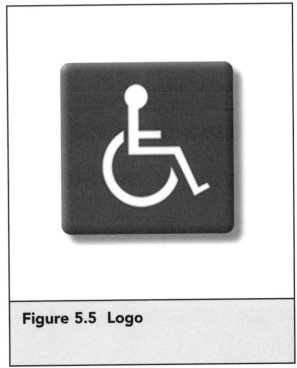

Figure 5.5 Logo

represents a person sitting in a wheelchair. A circle logo meaning "eat" somewhat resembles a plate, a relationship that could be perceived visually or through touch. The less the logo resembles what it refers to, the more abstract the symbol; the more it resembles its referent, the more iconic it is. However, a logo may closely resemble its referent when viewed visually but may not have any relationship to its referent when examined tactilely.

Line Drawings

Line drawings are black-and-white or color drawings of people, activities, animals, or items that visually depict their referents. Although line drawings closely resemble what they represent, they may

Figure 5.6 Line drawing: Apple

not be realistic and can be somewhat abstract depending on the intended message. A drawing of a cake to represent the word *cake* can be quite concrete and iconic, especially if it is a drawing of exactly the same kind of cake. Adding a specific color to a drawing—for example, a red apple versus a green apple—increases its visual similarity to the object it represents (see Figure 5.6). A drawing of two hands representing the manual sign for HELP is considerably more abstract. Drawings can be commercially made or homemade. The closer the visual similarity of the picture is to what it represents, the more iconic or concrete it is considered. Some children may more easily relate a line drawing to its referent if the referent (for example, a cookie) is used as a model to demonstrate how the line drawing is made (for example, by drawing around the cookie).

Photographs

Photographs can closely resemble what they are meant to represent and so are considered quite visually concrete in their representation (see Figure 5.7). A color photograph of a child's favorite toy reflects the same shape and color of the desired item, so the relationship is clear. However, when photographs contain multiple bits of information, or when they only tangentially refer to the referent, they may be more abstract. For example, a photo of a corner of the room with chairs, table, pictures, and toys can be used to mean "centers" in a classroom, or a photo of a CD being put into a computer can be used to mean "computer time." A photo of a restroom with rows of sinks, soap dispensers, mirrors, and the tile on the wall make the photograph more visually complex and difficult to discriminate than a photograph of a single sink and faucet to indicate "restroom break." Photographs with the same subject (for example, "dog") can be taken from different visual perspectives and may be more challenging for some children to identify.

Miniatures

Miniatures are very small items that are designed to "look like" certain referents; for example, a small elephant means "elephant." They can be handled and explored tactilely. When examined visually, they may closely approximate what they represent— a tiny house for a home or a plastic animal for a real animal. However, when examined tactilely, they are often quite abstract and do not provide accurate information about what they represent. Although miniatures may be very concrete representations for those children who have adequate vision, they can be completely unlike their referent and meaningless for children without functional vision. Consequently, miniatures should not be used in teaching children who are blind. This critical consideration should be used to determine their appropriateness for certain children with visual

Figure 5.7 Photo: "Can I have a drink?"

Figure 5.8 Miniature: "Can I have a drink?"

impairments. As shown in Figure 5.8, while the miniature wooden bottle can be recognized visually, it would be difficult to identify solely through tactile exploration.

Parts of Objects

Parts of objects can visually and tactilely resemble their referent very closely and as a result are considered concrete symbols. For example, a piece of a straw can represent "drink" *if* the child typically uses a straw to drink. Similarly, using a bottle top to indicate "drink" will only be meaningful if a child drinks from and has experience with bottles with this type of top (see Figure 5.9). Parts of objects as communication symbols can be large or small; however, the smaller the object part, the

easier it will be to display and to transport where it is needed. Parts of objects that are to be recognized tactilely should be based on meaningful tactile information from the child's perspective; for example, part of the handles from a bike can be used to represent "bike" because that's what the child feels when riding the bike. Parts of objects that are to be recognized visually should be selected based on clearly representative visual information; for example, the streamers hanging from the bike handles can be used to represent the bicycle visually. Parts of objects that are not easily seen or felt by the child will be more abstract and the relationship less clear.

Whole Objects

Whole objects are clearly concrete representations of their referent. A cup is used to mean "drink," a bottle for "milk," a toy ball for "playing ball," and so on. The object may or may not be used in the activity it represents; however, the association to the referent is very clear and, therefore, may be easier to learn. For example, a CD is clearly connected to "working on the computer" but is not necessarily used in the activity (see Figure 5.10).

DETERMINING COMMUNICATION MODES

Children with multiple disabilities may need certain modes for receptive

Figure 5.9   Part of object: "Can I have a drink?"

communication (for example, manual signs) and others (for example, objects) to express themselves. Modes may vary depending on whether the situation is familiar or unfamiliar, and the child's communication modes may change over time as the child increases his or her communication skills. As discussed in the previous chapter on tactile skills, communication modes should be selected based on the child's strengths and use of sensory information as well as the family and child's preferences. There are minimum basic skills that a child needs in order to use, receive, and understand tactile communication modes, including the ability to accept tactile input, to make minimal hand movements, to maintain physical contact

with an object or person for a few seconds, to keep his or her hands open, and to engage in active tactile exploration.

SELECTED TACTILE COMMUNICATION OPTIONS

Tactile communication options must be made highly salient to the child so that he or she can perceive them tactilely and associate them with their meaning. As an analogy, in a conversation, the sound "signal" (spoken word) must be detectable in the presence of "background noise" (other sounds that are unrelated to the speaker's message). Background noise can be decreased or the auditory signal can be made louder, or both. Similarly, a tactile "signal"—a touch cue, an object cue, a textured symbol, or a manual sign—should be easily separated from the "background noise"—other tactile input that is unrelated to the message. Tactile "signals" should provide very different and obvious tactile input from the "background noise" of daily care and other physical contact.

Children who have multiple disabilities and visual impairments need specific supports to develop receptive and expressive communication. As shown in Table 5.1, certain tactile communication options may be used for both receptive and expressive communication, whereas others are limited to communication input or output. This book addresses the most common

Figure 5.10 Whole object: "I want to work on the computer."

tactile communication methods that are currently used with children who are visually impaired and have additional significant disabilities. This chapter discusses touch cues, object cues, and textured symbols. Chapter 6 will describe adapted signs such as sign on body, coactive signs, and tactile signs.

Touch Cues

Much has been written about the use of *touch cues* with young children with visual impairments and additional disabilities (Alsop, 2002; Chen, 1999; Klein, Chen & Haney, 2000; Rowland, Schweigert & Prickett, 1995). Touch cues provide an early and simple means of receptive communication for a child who does not understand words. A touch cue is made in a consistent manner by touching the child's body, acting as a clear physical signal that is intended to convey a specific message and a variety of communication functions, such as a request or direction, information, praise, or greeting. There is no standardized system of touch cues. Some appear to be arbitrary—for example, to praise, encourage, or inhibit the child's action—whereas others have a direct relationship to the message that is being conveyed within the *specific* context. For example, at meal time, touching the child's mouth may be a request for the child to "take a bite." Touch cues that have a relationship to the activity or message

TABLE 5.1 TACTILE COMMUNICATION OPTIONS	
Tactile input/receptive communication	Output/expressive communication
Touch cues Signs on body	Facial expressions, body movements, touch
Object cues	Objects
Textured symbols	Textured symbols
Tactile signs	Coactive signs and spontaneous signs

may be easier for the child to understand than those that are more arbitrary, so these types of touch cues should be considered as a place to begin.

Touch cues should be developed and used consistently by communication partners to convey specific messages to an individual child. If not, people may use these tactile signals in different ways, and this variation will confuse the child. For example, tapping the child's shoulder might be a greeting or a request for the child to sit down. Children may also use touch to communicate—for example, they may touch someone to get attention or initiate an interaction or touch an object to indicate interest.

Touch cues signal the communicator's intent and may reduce a child's startle reflex or inappropriate behaviors elicited by sudden or confusing interactions. For example, touching the child under his or her elbows could signal, "I'm going to pick you up now," so the child is not startled by being picked up. Touch cues should be produced so that they are clear, emphatic, but gentle tactile signals (that is, that the child can easily discriminate them from other physical contact, for example, when the child is being positioned). As an analogy, it is easier for the child to hear what someone is saying to him or her if there are no competing or distracting sounds. Similarly, decrease or stop other competing physical contacts (for example, wiping the child's face) before giving the child the touch cue (for example,

a tap on mouth to signal "time to eat") so that he or she can attend to the cue and associate it with what is happening. Touch cues support a child's communication and participation in familiar routines. For instance, a caregiver can give a child a touch cue, then pause and wait for the child to indicate readiness or anticipation of the next step in the routine. When touch cues are used consistently during everyday activities, the child learns to recognize what they mean and can anticipate interaction. Three characteristics of touch cues differentiate them from signs made on the child's body (see discussion under "Signs on Body," Chapter 6); they are individualized for each child, their meaning is based on the context, and they are *not* symbols:

- Using gentle pressure to push down on the child's shoulder means "let's sit down here" (direction).

- Rubbing the child's right shoulder means "I like that" (praise).

- Touching the back of the child's hand means "Hi, here I am" (greeting).

- Touching the child's hair means "I'm going to brush your hair" (information).

Suggestions for Practice: Touch Cues

With all children with disabilities, particularly if a child has a severe neurological impairment, the type and placement of touch must be carefully selected. In most cases, a touch cue that is firm tends to be more acceptable to the child than a light stroke. The child's physical and occupational therapist should be consulted regarding the development and use of touch cues. Begin by selecting a few (3–5) touch cues that are very easy for the child to discriminate because they are made on different parts of his or her body (for example, on the chin, arm, hand, and foot). Once touch cues are selected for use with a particular child, practice them from the child's perspective. Close your eyes and have someone silently produce a touch cue on your body. What does that message convey? If the message seems clear, begin using the selected touch cues with the child and carefully observe his or her response.

Touch cues are easy for family members and service providers to develop and do not require very much formal instruction. These tactile signals are most appropriate for young children or older students who have significant and multiple disabilities. They can be tailored for each child who needs them. However, they are *limited* in the types of communication messages that they can convey—for example, letting the child know what is about to happen, providing comfort, praise, or encouragement, making a request, or giving a direction)—although the content of the message may vary. The specific content of

a request may be "Let's sit down" (tapping the child on the shoulder) or "Let's eat" (tapping the child on the lip twice). It is most important that communication partners agree upon selected touch cues that will be used accurately and consistently with an individual child. Otherwise, the child may be confused or startled by cues that are used in a haphazard manner. Touch cues should be considered as one of the possible options for providing communication input to a child who has significant disabilities. Consult "Using Touch Cues" for further guidance on the use of these cues.

The following vignette illustrates the selection and use of specific touch cues and other communication options to support interactions with an infant who has significant disabilities.

Vignette: Cassandra and Her Family

Ten-month-old Cassandra lives with her mother and grandfather. One of her favorite times of the day is when her mother holds her and slowly rocks in the recliner. Cassandra seems content, quiet, and alert during this slow rocking activity but will cry and fuss if she is rocked too fast or handled roughly. Her mother reports that she quiets when she is picked up and cries when left alone.

Cassandra has severe vision loss due to bilateral cataracts and glaucoma. She has light perception, a severe to profound bilateral hearing loss, microcephaly, and severe heart problems. She has not yet received hearing aids. Cassandra also has hypotonia and poor head control. She receives two visits a week from an early interventionist and a monthly visit from an occupational therapist. Cassandra does not grasp or otherwise handle or explore objects. Based on Casssandra's preferences, her service providers and family have developed a plan for using selected strategies within preferred activities as shown in Tables 5.2, 5.3, and 5.4. The example

---

USING TOUCH CUES

GUIDING QUESTIONS

1. Given the child's preferences and abilities, are touch cues an efficient and acceptable way to provide some communication input to this child?

2. If so, when are touch cues needed during the child's day?

3. What messages need to be communicated?

4. What touch cues are needed?

5. Who will use them?

6. How does the child respond to touch?

7. Can touch cues be provided clearly so the child does not confuse them with other prompts?

POINTS TO REMEMBER

- Be respectful.

- Touch the child on his or her body where it is socially acceptable and age-appropriate.

- Provide clear touch cues that are easy to discriminate.

- Remember that touch cues are not standardized.

- Use touch cues consistently.

shows selected cues and key signs, but Cassandra should also be exposed to language and conversations that occur during caregiver-infant interactions and early turn-taking exchanges.

Object Cues

An *object cue* is an object or part of an object that is used to represent a person, place, object, or activity and provides a concrete communicative exchange for the child who does not use abstract symbols. Initially, selected objects must be used in the activity in order for a child to understand what they represent. For instance, a spoon can be shown to the child to convey the message "time for a snack." If the snack is always eaten with a spoon, the child will eventually understand the meaning of the object cue; however, if the snack is typically finger food, then another object—for example, the wrapper of favorite crackers—should be used instead. The object cue lets the child know what is about to happen (for example, "We're going to have snack now"), provides a way for the child to understand what is expected (for example, "I need to go to the snack table"), and offers a means for the child to indicate requests or comments ("I want cookies" or "Cookies are my favorite snack"). Once the child understands the meaning of a specific object, make the object cue a bit more abstract or symbolic; that is, do not use the object that is used in the activity, but use a piece of an object. Begin to fade the use of concrete object cues and introduce more

TABLE 5.2 IDENTIFICATION CUES FOR CASSANDRA'S COMMUNICATION PARTNERS	
Cassandra's communication partners	Identification cue
Mother	Gently squeeze Cassandra's hands
Grandfather	Beard
Early interventionist	Medallion on necklace
Occupational therapist	Small Koosh ball

abstract object cues when the child consistently discriminates, recognizes, and understands the meaning of the concrete object cue.

The seminal work of Jan van Dijk introduced a systematic approach for communication with children who are deaf-blind by using *objects* to represent daily and

Activity	Strategy	Cassandra's responses that indicate understanding
Changing her diaper	• Help C. touch diaper wipes (object cue) • Let C. smell the wipes (olfactory cue)	• Touches or grasps wipes • Quiets and waits
Playing a rocking game	• Hold C. and sway back and forth before sitting in rocker (movement cue) • Pause in rocking game; help C. sign MORE (coactive sign) to resume the action	• Kicks legs • Gets excited • Rocks forward and back • Claps hands
Picking her up	• Gently pat C. under her arms (touch cue)	• Raises arms • Leans forward
Having a drink	• Stroke nipple of bottle on C.'s cheek (touch cue) • Sign EAT on C.'s mouth (sign on body)	• Moves head to nipple • Opens mouth
Ending an activity	• Tactilely sign FINISHED	• Pauses and waits

TABLE 5.3 SELECTED TACTILE STRATEGIES FOR INTERACTING WITH CASSANDRA

	TABLE 5.4 CASSANDRA'S ROCKING CHAIR GAME WITH MOM		
Tactile strategies	**Communication partner**	**Expectations of child**	**Response to child**
Touch identification cue	Gently squeeze C.'s hands and say, "Mama's here."	Attend to me.	Kiss C. on the forehead
Touch cue	Place hands under C.'s arms, lift up slightly then pause before picking her up.	Lean forward toward me.	Pick her up and say, "Up you go to the rocking chair." Hold her and move back and forth in rocking motion, then walk to the chair.
Touch cue	Sit in rocking chair with C. on lap and wait (delay strategy).	Smile, move body.	Touch her legs and say, "You want to rock? Rock, rock." Immediately start rocking in the chair.
Coactive sign	After rocking back and forth a few times, stop and wait for C.'s response (interruption strategy).	Move body.	"Want more rocking?" Help C. sign MORE coactively. Immediately start rocking.

TABLE 5.4 (CONTINUED)			
Mutual tactile attention	Carefully observe C.'s hand movements and join in her actions (for example, touching her shirt).	Accept my hands beside hers.	Follow C.'s lead and stop imitating her hand movements if she tires of the game.
Coactive sign	Carefully observe C.'s reactions.	Indicate the need to stop rocking.	Repeat rocking game three times or until C. tires of it. Say and coactively sign ALL DONE and get up from the chair.

memorable activities (van Dijk, 1966; 1986). Objects may be used to supplement spoken and signed communication for many different topics of conversations—for example, as a means of discussing preferences and interests, making comparisons, relating past events, and preparing for upcoming activities.

Research indicates the positive effects of systematic and meaningful instruction in teaching children and adolescents who have significant disabilities to communicate using tangible symbols. Rowland and Schweigert (2000) examined the use of tangible symbols such as objects, textures, and pictures by children with severe disabilities who lacked functional symbolic communication. Direct instruction involved approximately 15 minutes during each school day for an average of 6.5 months. Thirty-five of 41 children acquired the use of tangible symbols for expressive functional communication, and some progressed to using abstract symbols, including speech.

The literature in the field of deaf-blindness and visual impairments reveals a number of terms that have been used to refer to the use of objects as a communication means. The term "object of reference" is mainly found in publications from Europe and is used to differentiate between an *object cue*—the actual object that is used in the activity—and another object that is more symbolic because it is not actually used in the activity (Aitken et al., 2000; Best & Boothroyd, 1998). Objects as three-dimensional symbols are included under the category of "tangible symbols" (Rowland & Schweigert, 2000). In this book, the term "object cue," is used, whether it is the actual object used in the activity or a more abstract form of the object, because of its frequent use in the literature on deaf-blindness in the United States (Alsop, 2002; Chen, 1999; Rowland, Schweigert & Prickett, 1995).

There is no set number of object cues that should be introduced to a child. Begin by identifying a few activities that occur frequently and are very motivating to the child. Provide object cues that are associated with these highly preferred activities so the child can learn to use the objects to indicate choices, express desires, or initiate conversations. As with other communication options, speech and signs are also used as appropriate. The following are examples of how to use whole and partial objects as object cues:

Whole objects:

- A cup can represent "Snack time," "Let's go to the table," or "I'm thirsty."

- A backpack can represent "Here's the bus. Time for school" or "I want to go home."

- A seashell and some driftwood may be used in a tactile book to recount the trip to the beach.

- A candle and a party hat may be used to discuss plans for a birthday party.

Parts of objects:

- A section of a straw may represent "Snack time" or "I'm thirsty."

- The rubber grip of a bike handle could represent "Let's ride our bikes" or "I had fun riding my bike" (see Figure 5.11).

Figure 5.11 Object cue: Bike handle grip indicates going for a ride

- A piece of chain from the swing can mean "It's recess. I want to go on the swing" or "Let's go to the park."

Suggestions for Practice: Object Cues

First, consider whether the child has the physical ability to actively explore and manipulate objects to determine whether object cues provide appropriate communication cues for this child. Identify the types of objects that the child prefers to handle and explore during activities, and select object cues that meet these characteristics. The following are suggestions for how best to use object cues with children:

1. Begin with a limited number of objects to represent the child's preferred activities or key activities of the day. For example, Amy loves playing peek-a-boo with her mother, and a cotton scarf (object cue) represents this game; Leroy enjoys walking the dog with his big brother, and a leash (object cue) represents this afternoon outing. Key activities of the school day may be represented through an activity schedule (for example, going to school [backpack], snack time [lunch ticket], recess [wrist band], going home [backpack]).

2. Initially, the object cue can be the same object that is used in the actual activity so the child will easily understand its meaning. The child just needs to discriminate it from one or more other tangible symbols. The child will learn that "object A = activity A." Once the child associates the closely related object with the activity, a representative and more abstract object cue (not used in the activity) can be introduced.

3. When possible, choose small objects or parts of objects so the communication system is more portable. Select object cues that the child can easily discriminate and that have a close tactile relationship to their referents. *Avoid* the use of miniatures, because their relationships to referents are visually based.

4. Object cues should be organized and displayed so that they are accessible to the child and used consistently by communication partners (for example, in a calendar box for an activity schedule, on a communication board (see Figure 5.12), in a binder separated in categories, or as a landmark for the place to

Figure 5.12   Communication board for snack: Velcroed objects

which the object refers). Write the intended message clearly on the object or the material on which the object is mounted to clarify the communication intent for all communication partners. There are many helpful publications to assist in the development and implementation of tangible calendars, schedule books, or activity schedules (Alsop, 2002; Blaha, 2002, Downing & Peckham-Hardin, 2001; Rowland, Schweigert & Prickett, 1995).

Object cues provide a concrete and static communication method that may be easily understood by the child who does not use abstract symbols. They supplement and support symbolic communication. Object cues require a simple motor response on the part of the child, such as pointing, touching, grasping, picking up, showing, looking at them, or going to the place or activity they represent. They make relatively low demands on the child's cognition, memory, and representational skills

---

USING OBJECT CUES

GETTING STARTED

- Examine the child's daily routine and preferred activities and identify the object cues that are needed to represent selected activities.

- Select objects from the child's tactile perspective (that is, based on the child's experience). For example, an object cue for recess may be a piece of chain that represents a swing, because the child holds onto the chains of the swing.

- At first, start with a reasonable number of object cues (2–5) and add more as the child begins to show an understanding of what they represent.

POINTS TO REMEMBER

- Select objects that are relevant, easy to recognize, and interesting to the child.

- Create conversations through mutual tactile attention and tactile modeling by using objects with the child.

- Use the object with the activity it represents by introducing the object at the beginning of the activity, during the activity as part of the conversation, and at the end of the activity to signal that the activity is over.

and provide an option for communication input and output. As with other cue systems, they should be used correctly and consistently by everyone who interacts with the child. As discussed in Chapter 8 on Emergent Literacy, objects may be used to create conversations about an activity or a child's experience and used to develop books that promote the child's literacy skills. See "Using Object Cues" for more tips. The following vignette illustrates the use of a number of object cues and other communication options with a kindergartner who had multiple disabilities.

Vignette: Sally

Sally and her twin sister Yvonne attend kindergarten at their neighborhood school. Their parents are pleased that both girls go to the same school. The twins were born prematurely, and Sally was diagnosed with retinopathy of prematurity in the first few months of life. She has light perception, mild cerebral palsy, and developmental delays. Sally is nonverbal but makes her preferences known by smiling and vocalizing. She loves movement activities such as riding in a wagon with Yvonne, swinging on a swing, or splashing in the pool. She walks with support using a walker. When offered toys or other objects, she usually grabs them and either throws them behind her or bangs them on a nearby surface unless she is given support at the wrist or elbow to engage in handling and

exploration. For example, with support, she can place balls in a plastic container that plays music when a ball is dropped in it or poke and pat Play-Doh. Sally also responds to singing, sound games, and the sounds of musical instruments. She has been observed imitating animal sounds such as "moo" during music time and creative play activities. Sally's educational team includes a teacher credentialed in visual impairments, an inclusion specialist, and a speech and language pathologist.

The team met to plan the use of tactile strategies with Sally. They wanted to create an activity schedule using objects for the school's routine, decide on identification cues for classmates and service providers, and identify cues and signs that would be used frequently to support her expressive communication along with the use of a voice output device. Although Sally does not have a hearing loss, her response to speech is inconsistent, and her understanding of spoken words is unclear, so other communication methods are being used as well as speech and voice output systems. Tables 5.5, 5.6, and 5.7 contain suggestions for selected identification and object cues and signs during routine activities to supplement conversations with a child such as Sally who is blind and has additional disabilities. Sally should also participate in a rich language environment derived from the context of and mutual tactile attention in social interactions.

TABLE 5.5 IDENTIFICATION CUES FOR SALLY'S COMMUNICATION PARTNERS

Sally's communication partners	Identification cues
Dora (classmate)	Eyeglasses
Teacher	Wrist watch
Classroom assistant	Sign M (for Mary) on Sally's body
Teacher of students with visual impairments	Jumbo braille brooch
Speech and language pathologist	Tap fingers on Sally's palm

TABLE 5.6 OBJECT CUES FOR SCHOOL ACTIVITY SCHEDULE

Activity	Object
Morning circle	Piece of carpet
Reading center	Piece of braille book (although Sally does not yet read braille)
Math center	Plastic pegs for counting
Art center	Pipe cleaners or clay (change based on art project)
Music center	Small rhythm instrument
Library	Audio tape
Computer	CD
Physical education	Small bean bag
Snack	Empty snack bag
Bathroom	Small tile
Recess	Chain (for swing)

TABLE 5.7 SALLY AND DORA READ TOGETHER AT SCHOOL			
Tactile strategies	Communication partner	Expectations of child	Response to child
Object cue	Teacher offers S. a choice between "reading corner" and "computer" using a piece of paper with braille and a CD.	Handle the braille paper and CD with support at the wrist. S. is likely to choose reading, because the braille paper is easier to grasp and S. enjoys reading with a classmate, Dora.	Teacher responds, "OK, you want to read with Dora." Teacher helps S. push her walker to the book area and sit on the sofa.
Hand-under-hand guidance Object identification cue	Dora touches S.'s hands, says, "Hi Sally," and uses hand-under-hand to guide S. to touch her glasses.	Feel Dora's glasses, smile, and vocalize.	
Tactile signing	Dora offers a book of animals to S., places it on her lap, and tactilely signs BOOK.	S. tolerates the book on her lap, touches the book, taps the page, and searches for a button.	Teacher encourages S. to open the book and to press a button by prompting her at the wrist.
Mutual tactile attention	Dora places her hand beside S.'s, imitates S.'s hand movements, and imitates animal sounds.	Imitate animal sounds. Grasp the tip of pages or pat pages and turn her head toward sound.	Teacher imitates animal sounds with children

CONTINUED ON NEXT PAGE

TABLE 5.7 (CONTINUED)			
Tactile strategies	Communication partner	Expectations of child	Response to child
Physical prompt	Teacher uses wrist prompts to encourage S. to turn the pages. Dora and S. take turns pressing buttons.	Keep hand on teacher's and imitate sounds. Keep hands close to Dora's, take turns, and then grasp the closed book.	Teacher labels animals using tactile sign and speech and makes animal sounds until the book ends.
Tactile signing	Dora says and tactilely signs BOOK FINISH and closes the book.	S. takes the book to the shelf.	Teacher says and tactilely signs PUT BOOK ON SHELF.

Selected Tactile Strategies

In addition to a variety of touch cues, object cues, and tactile signs as shown in the previous tables, other tactile strategies may be used with children like Sally. *Mutual tactile attention* encourages interactions between children, and *hand-under-hand guidance* and *tactile modeling* support manipulation and exploration of objects. For example, a classmate invites Sally to play the piano by placing his or her hand right beside Sally's and imitating her hand movements (mutual tactile attention). The teacher encourages Sally to learn different ways to play with Play-Doh by placing her hands on top of those of another child who is demonstrating how to roll the Play-Doh (tactile modeling).

Textured Symbols

Textured symbols are tactilely salient, three-dimensional artificial representations associated with people, objects, and activities and used for receptive and expressive communication. These symbols are individualized for each child and could be abstract (unrelated to the referent) or iconic (closely related to the referent). They provide a portable means of receptive and expressive communication for a child who does not use sign, speech, or graphic modes.

Textured symbols have been used successfully with older students who are deaf-blind and have very limited use of other communication methods (Murray-Branch

SUGGESTIONS FOR THE USE OF TEXTURED SYMBOLS

Identify whether textured symbols are an efficient means of receptive and expressive communication for an individual child. If so, create conversations through mutual tactile attention and tactile modeling by using selected textured symbols with the child. The following considerations are suggested by Murray-Branch & Bailey (1998):

1. Select textures for symbols based on the child's preferences and ability to discriminate them. Selected textures must be tactilely salient (easy to recognize) and distinctive from each other. They should maintain their saliency and surface uniformity when reduced in size and regardless of orientation.

2. Each textured symbol should have its intended message written clearly on it to clarify the communication intent for all communication partners.

3. Select a highly reinforcing and very specific referent (for example, graham crackers). Introduce the texture (for example, a square covered with dried glue dots) that represents the referent during consistent routines (for example, at snack time). Present this symbol every time the child can have the desired item.

4. Start with a large presentation of the texture (for example, 8" x 10") so the child can easily touch it. Begin with an action that the child can produce (for example, putting his or her hand on the texture). Give the child the actual referent whenever he or she makes any contact, accidental or intentional, with the textured symbol. When the child consistently touches the symbol, reduce the size of the texture. Individual needs and abilities will decide the ultimate size of the texture.

5. Introduce each texture symbol by itself. Once the child understands the meaning of this new symbol, it can be used with others to offer a choice.

6. A symbol without a referent can be used as a foil in teaching the child to make a choice. A foil is usually a smooth flat square the same size as the other textures. If the child selects a foil, it means nothing, so gently guide the child's hand to the display area so he can choose a texture that has a referent. Over time, the child will attend more to the textures that have a clear referent.

7. Increase the number of textured symbols to represent different referents that are appropriate for the child's use.

& Bailey, 1998). Murray-Branch, Udvari-Solner & Bailey (1991) evaluated the use of textured symbols with two students (15 and 23 years old) who were deaf-blind and had severe cognitive disabilities and very limited expressive communication. Textured symbols were developed according to the individual's preferences and abilities and introduced through systematic instruction. After approximately three months of instruction during naturally occurring opportunities, both students demonstrated use of multiple textured symbols to make requests and indicate choices. The following are examples of textured symbols:

- A piece of artificial turf represents "recess."

- A piece of cardboard with hardened glue dots represents "chocolate pudding."

- A piece of rubber material from a swim cap represents "Let's go swimming."

A textured symbol can be easily recognized tactilely without significant manual exploration if the texture is salient (for example, 1/4-inch bumps made by hardened glue 1/2 inch apart on cardboard or a piece of bubble wrap packaging sheet). Because the texture is uniform across the surface area, the textured symbol does *not* have to be presented in a particular orientation, and the child does not need to have a reference point from which to tactilely examine the symbol. On the other hand, textured symbols do not necessarily possess the attributes of the referents they represent or have a clear perceptual relationship to their referents. Textured symbols may be used for communication input and output with children who have multiple disabilities. See "Suggestions for the Use of Textured Symbols" for more tips.

SUMMARY

Communication is the key to helping the child understand the world around him or her. The child receives different tactile information as receptive communication and can use a variety of behaviors to send a message expressively. Several examples were provided in this chapter as means to supporting receptive and expressive communication. The most effective communicative strategies are individually determined for each child based upon a number of unique characteristics. There is no need to decide on one option to use with a child; rather, take advantage of the different possibilities. The goal is to make communicative interactions as clear as possible. The next chapter presents the use of manual signs as an additional mode for tactile interactions.

Chapter 6

Adapting Manual Signs to Meet a Child's Needs

For children who have both vision and hearing losses, American Sign Language is not an accessible communication system, as it is primarily visual and highly abstract. This chapter shows how these manual signs can be adapted to become an important communication option for children with visual impairments or who are deaf-blind and may have additional physical and cognitive needs.

AMERICAN SIGN LANGUAGE

American Sign Language (ASL) is a visually based language system that is the natural language of deaf people who belong to what is considered Deaf culture in the United States. Deaf children of deaf parents learn ASL during their early years, just as hearing children learn speech in their hearing families. It is a language with its own syntax and grammatical rules that differ from those of English. The phonology of ASL is composed of four complex parameters: the receiver sees and identifies the manual signs that a signer produces based on their hand shape or configuration,

the orientation of the hands in relationship to the body, the movement of the hands from one point to another, and the location on the body where the sign is produced or place of articulation in space (Fisher & Siple, 1990; Klima & Bellugi, 1979). Sign systems such as *Signing Exact English* (SEE) and other manual codes for English are based on English syntax and use some ASL signs (Vernon & Andrews, 1990). These systems are used in educational programs to support the child's development of English skills such as speech, reading, and writing.

Research indicates that acquisition of signs depends on the degree of perceptual salience of a sign and the association between the sign and its meaning that will assist in the recall of the sign (Griffith & Robinson, 1980; Griffith, Robinson & Panagos, 1983). Such associations may not be based on a physical resemblance between the sign and its referent but are influenced by the person's experience. In a study of tactile iconicity of signs, Griffith, Robinson, and Panagos (1983) found that signs rated as highly iconic by sighted and hearing children and adults and deaf adults were also tactilely perceived as iconic by adults who were blind. The degree of iconicity of manual signs seems to predict the ease of their acquisition by children who have intellectual impairments (Griffith & Robinson, 1980). These researchers concluded that highly iconic signs are easier to learn because they are representations of highly salient concepts, and they look like and feel like the actions or objects they represent. Findings suggest that an initial sign vocabulary should focus on concepts that are the most meaningful to the child who has multiple disabilities and requires an alternative mode of communication.

Kahn's (1996) study of 34 children with severe and profound intellectual impairments who were being taught manual signs found that few of these children used signs expressively. Findings suggest that children need to display a certain level of cognitive functioning before successful acquisition of abstract signs can occur. In addition, findings highlight the importance of children using signs throughout the day and across different activities, not only during direct instruction, if they are to generalize the use and meaning of these signs.

ADAPTING MANUAL SIGNS

The use of manual signs has been adapted to meet the learning needs of children with disabilities who have limited means of communication. When a child has both a visual impairment and hearing loss, appropriate adaptations to signs will be needed to meet the child's visual and tactile means of obtaining information (Blaha & Carlson, 1996; Thestrup & Anderson, 1994). This section discusses three adaptations that are commonly used with children who are deaf-blind or who are blind with multiple disabilities: making the sign on a child's body, helping the child to sign coactively (that is, guiding the child to produce the sign), and producing signs that the child can receive tactilely.

It is important to differentiate between the input and output purposes of these adapted signs. If a communication partner produces a sign on the child's body (input), then the child is the receiver. If a communication partner helps the child to sign coactively (output), then the child is the sender. In tactile signing, the sender (communication partner) produces signs, and the receiver (child) places his or her hand(s) on the sender's hand(s) to receive the message (input). Whenever the conventional use of manual signs is adapted for a child's vision loss, the child must have additional opportunities to tactilely perceive all four parameters that distinguish one sign from another—hand shape, orientation, location, and movement. Without this exposure, the child's discrimination, recognition, and comprehension of a sign and its meaning will be severely limited or inaccurate. Figures 6.1 through 6.3 show examples of adapting the conventional sign for SLIDE to sign on body (Figure 6.1 and Figure 6.2) and tactile sign (Figure 6.3). The child must have sufficient physical movement and dexterity to produce a sign coactively and to discriminate and recognize tactile signs.

Given that manual signs were developed as an effective means of visual communication, tactile adaptations of a visual system should be carefully planned and implemented, particularly when children are just beginning to acquire language. Each child's team of service providers and family should evaluate the effectiveness of adapted signs as an efficient communication method for the individual child who is deaf-blind. Hearing communication partners should continue to speak naturally to the child while using adapted signs to preserve the natural quality of interactions and to provide additional auditory language input that a child may understand if he or she has some hearing.

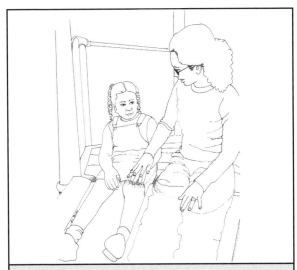

Figure 6.2   Complete sign on body: SLIDE

Figure 6.1   Begin sign on body: SLIDE

Figure 6.3   Tactile sign: SLIDE

Signs on Body

The term "signs on body" is defined as a standard manual sign that a signer produces directly on the receiver's body. These adaptations have been also called "body-based signs" and "body signs." There is some debate among service providers in the United States as to whether this tactile adaptation of manual signs is a true symbol or merely a touch cue. Signs on body have been used to support the development of receptive communication with children who are deaf-blind and may be unable to see signs produced visually and may have difficulty perceiving tactile signs (Chen, 1999; Joint, 1998). In Australia and Scotland, body signs have been used extensively with children who are deaf-blind or blind with significant disabilities (Joint, 1998; Lee & MacWilliam, 2002).

Research indicates that deaf mothers naturally make some signs directly on their babies' bodies (Maestas Y Moores, 1980; Spencer, 1991; Spencer, Bodner-Johnson & Gutfreund, 1992), and this tactile interaction serves to engage the infant's attention and joint focus with the parent. Some family members and service providers of children who are deaf-blind have adapted signs to make them on the child's body.

Deaf infants, sighted infants, and children who have low vision can see all four parameters of the sign (hand configuration, orientation, placement, and movement) because they can see the sign when it is produced conventionally. When a signer produces a sign on a child's body, the signer is communicating through symbols. If a signer produces a sign on the body of a child who cannot see it, the child will perceive the *placement* and perhaps the movement of the sign—similar to a touch cue—but will not have access to information about the *hand orientation* or configuration (features of the symbol). Therefore, it is critical that this child is exposed to other uses of manual signs (that is, coactive and tactile signing and visual manual signs if appropriate) in order to build his or her recognition of these symbols and their meanings. The following are examples of how manual signs may be produced as signs on a child's body:

- STAND: Signer places the tips of his or her index and middle fingers on the child's palm (child feels two static pressure points on his or her palm).

- TIME FOR BED: Signer places his or her palm on child's cheek (child feels a hand placed on his or her cheek).

- BATH: Signer rubs the knuckles of his or her fists ("A" hand shapes) against child's chest (child feels rubbing movement against his or her chest).

There are certain limitations to using signs on body as a receptive mode of communication. Not all manual signs can be converted to signs on body—only those that involve hand shapes that are placed on the body, not those that are articulated in space. Some signs are produced on certain body areas that may be socially "off limits" to service providers (for example, BATH on the chest of an older girl). As discussed previously, a child who is blind is likely to perceive a sign made on his or her body by another as a touch cue. For example, as shown in Figures 6.4 and 6.5, the signs CANDY and VEGETABLE have the same placement (touch cheek), orientation, and movement (rotate hand clockwise and counter clockwise while in contact with the cheek), and differ only in the parameter of hand configuration ("V" and "1" hand shapes, respectively). The child will perceive a rotating pressure point from a finger on his or her cheek for both these signs. The child can gain a symbolic understanding of the sign only if encouraged to use his or her hand to feel the hand shape of the sign being made on the body. Otherwise, the child may become frustrated and confused regarding this sign on body and the anticipated outcome. Additional exposure to signs through coactive or tactile signing is essential to learn about the two other parameters of the sign: hand configuration and orientation. See "Suggestions for the Use of Sign on Body" for additional tips.

CANDY

Index finger on cheek, twist hand

Figure 6.4 Manual sign: CANDY

Signing Exact English illustrations supplied by Modern Signs Press, Inc.

VEGETABLE

Index fingertip of V on cheek; twist

Figure 6.5 Manual sign: VEGETABLE

Signing Exact English illustrations supplied by Modern Signs Press, Inc.

SUGGESTIONS FOR THE USE OF SIGN ON BODY

The following are suggestions for using signs on body:

1. Decide whether making signs on the child's body will support the child's receptive communication—whether they will be confusing or clarifying to the child—and whether the child will accept or reject this tactile interaction. This process requires careful observation of the child's reactions to signs made on his or her body.

2. Select a few signs and determine how they will be made on the child's body. If possible, practice making the sign on someone else and getting feedback.

3. Make the sign touch the child's body where the child would typically produce the sign if using it expressively. For example, sign MOTHER by touching the child's chin with the thumb of your "5" hand shape (see Figure 5.3 in Chapter 5). The child feels a thumb press on his or her chin.

4. In most cases, a sign on body that involves a firm touch (STAND involves two firm pressure points on the palm) may be easy for the child to perceive. Begin by using a few signs that are made on very different parts of the child's body (for example, on the arm and the face) so they are easy for the child to discriminate. Signs on body also must be easily differentiated from other physical contact (for example, touch cues or body positioning).

5. Whenever possible, encourage the child to touch the signer's hand or hands as the sign is being made on the child's body so that he or she will tactilely perceive all features of the manual sign (See Figure 6.6: Sign on body: CANDY).

6. If a child has a severe neurological impairment, the way the sign is produced on the child's body—the type of touch and hand placement and movement—must be evaluated and the child's physical and occupational therapists should be consulted. Selected signs made on the child's body should *not* elicit reflex reactions or cause the child to startle.

> *"People who really understand communication almost do signs on the body naturally, and people who wouldn't do them naturally, [may not] understand how and why to do them at all."*
>
> —M. Belote

Signs on body are different from *touch cues* because they are standard manual signs that are produced on the child's body. *Signs on body* represent words and are abstract symbols, and *touch cues* are individualized signals or prompts that are made on the child's body. As one professional notes:

A child may perceive and recognize signs made on his or her body since they involve a single and distinct touch and movement. In contrast, *coactive signs* and *tactile signs* involve multiple touches and movements and are far more complicated to decipher for a young child who is learning how to communicate through touch. [S. Joint, personal communication, February 24, 2003]

Signs on body may also be used with children who have low vision. If a child can see manual signs but has difficulty visually tracking certain signs, these signs and other key words may be signed on the child's body, as Rafalowski Welch explains:

I have used a variation of signs on body with a boy who had a very limited visual field. He would visually track my signing, but when a sign would disappear from his view, I would make the sign on his body (for example, the sign for DOG). [T. Rafalowski Welch, personal communication, August 24, 2004]

The use of signs on body facilitates contact and communication with the child and helps prepare him or her for other forms of tactile communication (for example, coactive or tactile signs). Some children may be more receptive to having signs made on their bodies than having their hands manipulated through sign movements (coactive signs) or putting their hands over the signer's hands (tactile signs). In addition, signs can be made on the child's body while the child is examining an object, engaging in an activity, or

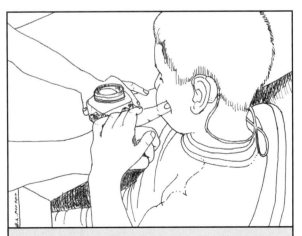

Figure 6.6 Sign on body: CANDY

demonstrating an emotion, allowing the meaning of the sign to be connected simultaneously with the referent without interrupting the child's focus of attention, activity, or hand use. Signs on body as an adapted sign approach is one tactile communication option that may be appropriate along with other communication options to support the communication development of an individual child.

The following are key points to keep in mind when using signs on a child's body:

- Be respectful in your interactions with the child and respond to his or her signals.

- Produce signs on the child's body only if this strategy is effective in meeting the child's learning needs and is an efficient mode of communication.

- Help the child obtain tactile information about the hand shape and other characteristics of the sign by allowing time for the child to explore the hand shape and encouraging this exploration.

Coactive Signing

Coactive signing is derived from van Dijk's terminology "coactive movement" or moving together (Alsop, 2002; MacFarland,

1995; van Dijk, 1966). A sign is produced with a child coactively (that is, by physically guiding the child's hand or hands to facilitate production of a standard manual sign for expressive communication). The intent of coactive signing is to help a child who is deaf-blind to produce signs and to develop *interactive signing* (the back and forth tactile signing used by adults who are deaf-blind) (Watkins & Clark, 1991). The following are examples of the use of coactive signing:

- Three-year-old Mariko is sitting in the swing. She shakes her legs when the swing stops. Her big brother takes her hands, helps to mold them into "flat O" hand shapes, and taps them together, producing the sign MORE while saying, "OK, you want to swing some more. I'll push you."

- Ten-year-old Carlos is sitting at the lunch table. He searches for his milk carton on the tray but cannot find it, so he touches his teacher. She takes Carlos's hand and guides him to sign MILK (C hand shape closes to S hand shape) *coactively* and then says, "The milk is on the counter, go get it," while she signs MILK ON COUNTER GET IT as Carlos feels her hand movements (tactile signing).

The SKI*HI Institute conducted an extensive national project to develop videotapes of coactive signs (Watkins & Clark, 1991). This project identified a list of 400 of the most frequently used words based on a literature review and input from INSITE home advisors (early interventionists in states that have adopted the Project INSITE model of home-based intervention for young children with sensory impairments and multiple disabilities) and state technical assistance deaf-blind projects. Seventy-two (18%) of these 400 signs were modified to make them tactilely salient, tactilely iconic, and easy to produce. A prototype videotape with a sample coactive sign lesson was field-tested with 150 parents and professionals in the United States and Canada. Modified signs were evaluated by deaf and hearing ASL users to determine whether they were recognizable as ASL signs. Very few were rated as unrecognizable. The project produced a series of videotapes of coactive signs that were selected because of function, tactile salience, iconicity, and ease of production.

Coactive signs may support the expressive communication of children who are visually impaired or who are not visually attentive but can perceive signs tactilely. They provide the child with a tactile-kinesthetic model for promoting expressive communication. Coactive signs may not be effective for children who do not like their hands to be held and manip-

ulated or who have limited arm and hand movements. As Joint observes,

> Having someone close behind them to facilitate coactive signing may be intimidating or confusing for some children. They may feel as if their hands are being manipulated too much. Service providers have found that if a child does not understand the purpose of coactive signing, he or she may interrupt the interaction and arch backwards to reject the person who is facilitating the production of coactive signs. [S. Joint, personal communication, February 24, 2003]

Coactive signs should be produced from the child's perception as the signer. If a communication partner is positioned in front of the child while assisting the child to sign coactively, care is needed to help the child produce the signs accurately and appropriately. Some communication partners may reverse the direction and movements of a sign and produce the sign from their own perspectives and not from the child's perspective. This will confuse the child. Initially, when coactive signing is used, some children may produce less than accurate signs (for example, with errors in hand configuration and movement) because they dislike having their hands molded into a shape or because the movements of some manual signs are difficult to produce (for example, signs that require finger movements, such as WAIT). At first, these early signing attempts should be accepted so that the child will quickly learn that his or her communication obtains a response. However, more accurate signs should be encouraged as the child increases his or her use of manual signs. Physical guidance in producing coactive signs should be decreased as soon as possible so that a child does not become dependent on physical prompts to produce signs. For more discussion, see the section on "Hand-over-Hand Guidance" in Chapter 4.

At the same time, the child should also be exposed to tactile signs or the visual signs as appropriate for his or her abilities. Children may have difficulty differentiating between messages from a communication partner (input) and the communication partner's efforts to facilitate the child's response (output). If a child is guided to use coactive signs to both receive messages (receptive) and to send messages (expressive), he or she will have difficulty differentiating turns in the conversation and initiating signed communication. See "Suggestions for the Use of Coactive Signs" for more tips on introducing coactive signs.

Tactile Signing

Manual signs are used tactilely with individuals who are deaf-blind, usually as a means of receptive communication (Harlin, 1996; Prickett, 1995). *Tactile signing* is a communication method based on a

standard manual sign system in which the receiver's hand or hands are placed lightly upon the hand or hands of the signer to perceive the signs. In this way, language in the form of manual signs is made accessible to children who are deaf and have insufficient vision to perceive signs visually. It is important to encourage young children who are blind and have a hearing loss to "listen" and participate in conversations by placing their hands on the signer's hands. Children need many opportunities to tactilely "follow" the hand movements of the signer's hands through physical contact in order to understand the meaning of the tactile signs and to produce signs expressively. Hearing children babble using their voices because they are continuously exposed to speech; similarly, deaf children of deaf parents "babble" using their hands because they are in a signing environment (Petitto & Marentette, 1991). Similarly, very young children who are deaf-blind need access to the language environment through tactile signing so that they can develop "babbling" and hand play that will promote their production of signs and language development. Here are some examples of how to introduce tactile signs:

- BALL: Claw hands to form a ball shape. Child places his or her hands on the signer's hands.

- DRINK: Place right "C" hand shape in front of the mouth, palm

SUGGESTIONS FOR THE USE OF COACTIVE SIGNS

The following are suggested methods for successfully introducing coactive signs:

1. Carefully observe the child's communicative behaviors (for example, facial expressions, body movements, gestures, and vocalizations) to identify the child's purposes or functions of these nonverbal communication behaviors.

2. Decide whether to use coactive signs to support the child's expressive communication. Is signing the most efficient way for this child to communicate? Does he or she need to be physically guided to produce the signs?

3. If coactive signs are to be used, identify *when* they should be used to expand the child's communicative means. For example, the child pushes dish away to indicate refusal, so the communication partner assists the child to sign FINISH coactively.

4. Introduce coactive signs for key words to express communicative behavior that is within the child's repertoire; for example, signals, gestures, and object cues.

5. Differentiate between communication input to the child and the output of the child, and use coactive signs only to facilitate the child's expressive communication (output).

6. The person who facilitates the child's coactive signs and the child should be positioned so that they are both comfortable and able to produce signs together. Because this person's position may vary in spatial relationship to the child (that is, beside the child, in front of the child, or behind the child), he or she should remember to facilitate sign production *from the child's perspective* (that is, use the child's dominant hand as the moving hand in producing the sign). The person's position in relationship to the child must be considered.

7. Pay attention to the specific parameters of the sign (that is, hand configuration, orientation, movement, and placement) and guide the child to produce the sign accurately.

8. Observe the child's reactions to coactive signs and decrease the amount of physical guidance as soon as the child begins to initiate the sign movements. For example, for the sign COOKIE, help position the child's open left hand while prompting him or her at the right elbow to tap his or her right fingers on the left palm. The goal is for the child to eventually produce the COOKIE sign in response to a natural cue (for example, smelling a cookie or wanting a cookie).

facing left, and make a motion as if taking a drink. Child places his or her hands on the signer's hands and follows the signer's movements.

See "Suggestions for the Use of Tactile Signing" for more ideas about introducing tactile signing.

The use of tactile signs provides a method of symbolic receptive communication for children who are deaf-blind. *Tactile signing* can lead to *interactive signing*, in which the child takes a turn in the conversation. Miles suggests, "One can easily encourage this by signing hand-under-hand to a child and then gently placing one's own hands on a young child's hands and waiting, as if to 'listen' for the child's turn. After a while this cueing is not necessary—the child begins to understand that he or she can also sign back" (personal communication, August 24, 2004).

Not all manual signs can be adapted easily to a tactile mode, and some signs may be more complicated to understand tactilely than visually. Modifications of standard signs of ASL or manual codes of English signs should be kept to a minimum so that the child will learn standard signs and will be able to communicate with other sign users. Tactile signs require the receiver to know how to position his or her hand(s) over the sender's hand(s). Therefore, tactile signing may not be useful for infants and other children because of physical, behavioral, or cognitive abilities

that make it difficult for them to actively obtain information in this manner. Further, the smaller hands of a child may not be able to accurately perceive the movements of the larger hands of adults who are producing signs.

Tactile signing should be used appropriately within activities to avoid interrupting the child's attention. For example, a teacher produces a sign that a child receives tactilely, and then the child begins the activity. To maintain communication, the teacher interrupts this child to provide sign input that the child receives tactilely. This interruption removes the child's hands from direct involvement with materials, potentially confusing the child. As with all other adapted signs, tactile signing should be used with speech and other communication options as appropriate to support the child's communication.

Vignette: Manuel

The following vignette demonstrates the use of key adapted signs of different types during routine activities to supplement conversations with a child who is deaf-blind. A few selected signs and object cues are also shown in the example, with the assumption that the child is exposed to a rich language environment that is derived from the context and mutual attention in social interactions.

Eleven-year-old Manuel recently joined a new foster family and is quite

SUGGESTIONS FOR THE USE OF TACTILE SIGNING

The following are suggested methods for successfully introducing tactile signing:

1. Consider the child's ability to place his or her hand(s) on the signer's hand(s) and to tactilely discriminate the specific parameters of the sign (that is, hand configuration, orientation, movement, and placement) to determine whether tactile signing is an appropriate method for the child's receptive communication.

2. Encourage the child to rest his or her hands lightly on the signer's; it takes time to learn to how to do this.

3. Identify where and when tactile signs could be beneficial for a particular child. What communication modes are most effective for supporting the child's receptive communication? Does the child have sufficient functional vision to perceive manual signs visually? In what situations does the child need to perceive signs tactilely?

Figure 6.7 Tactile sign: EAT

4. Introduce signs for key words to label communicative behavior that is within the child's repertoire (for example, signals, gestures, and object cues). If the child recognizes his or her spoon as a cue for mealtime, then sign EAT (see Figure 6.7), or if the child rocks his or her body when the swing stops, then sign MORE (see Figure 6.8).

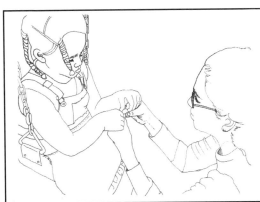

Figure 6.8 Tactile sign: MORE

5. Begin with signs for key words that are useful, used frequently,

CONTINUED ON NEXT PAGE

motivating, easy to make, easy to discriminate, and easily understood by the child. Determine the motor complexity of sign production and whether manual signs will be an effective means of communication for a child with physical disabilities. Consult an occupational or physical therapist if the child has motor problems.

6. B. Miles suggests that the child's communication partner "sign the names of objects, actions, activities, and feelings that are being shared during times of mutual tactile attention. Remember that a hearing child hears thousands, and perhaps millions of words before saying his or her first words, so a child who is deaf-blind needs many, many, repeated exposures to meaningful signs before he or she should be expected to understand or produce signs expressively" (personal communication, February 15, 2005).

7. Create multiple opportunities for the child to associate the tactile sign with the referent—the object, person, activity, or experience—so he or she can learn the meaning of the tactile sign. Provide opportunities for the child to generalize the meaning of tactile signs across activities, settings, and people.

8. Adapt standard signs and their pace of production as needed to make them easier to detect tactilely. However, be selective in adapting standard manual signs so that children can still communicate with a larger group of sign users.

9. Help the child understand the give-and-take of the communication process (that is, who is producing the sign and who is receiving the sign). The child needs to learn that when he or she perceives a sign tactilely, he or she is receiving a message, and the sender is waiting for his or her response. Build on nonsymbolic turn-taking games (for example, pat-a-cake) so that the child has repeated opportunities for engaging in the give-and-take of an interaction.

10. The communication partner and child should be positioned so that they are both comfortable and able to produce and receive signs. Because the communication partner's position may vary in relationship to the child (that is, beside or in front of the child), he or she should remember to facilitate the child's access to signed communication.

11. Some children will need tactile signs in some situations but not in others. For example, to follow the fast pace of signing, the child might choose to use

---

SUGGESTIONS FOR THE USE OF TACTILE SIGNING (CONTINUED)

touch and not vision, or the child may choose to use both depending on lighting conditions.

12. The use of tactile tracking helps a child with a reduced visual field to know where the signer's hands are in space and where to look. Tactile tracking involves touching the back of the signer's hands at the wrist.

13. Help the child understand the meaning of signs by signing about what you are experiencing together (see section on "Mutual Tactile Attention" in Chapter 4).

14. Some children will need individual support to use their communication system in a classroom where the teacher cannot convey information to the child individually.

---

comfortable in his new home. He interacts with people and objects by touching them lightly and seems to use his sense of smell and touch to recognize people. Manuel can see light, shadows, and the silhouettes of people and objects. He has a profound hearing loss and does not wear any amplification. He loves animals, so he helps feed and walk the family dog. Every evening, Manuel rolls along in his wheelchair while walking the dog with his foster father. He also enjoys horseback riding once a week at a local stable.

The family met with his teacher and other service providers to identify tactile communication methods that they could use at home. When Manuel wants something, he uses his object communication system on his wheelchair tray to express his need. For example, when he wants to drink juice, he finds the straw and taps on it. He understands a variety of object cues—a small piece of foam for bedtime, a piece of a leash for walking the dog, and coins with a wallet for buying a snack. He is starting to choose between two activities—a high- and a low- preference activity. He understands some of the signs that are tactilely signed to him (for example, DOG, EAT, FINISH, WALK, HORSE, RIDE, MORE, NO), and he is starting to sign FINISH and EAT with an elbow prompt (see Figure 6.9 for an example of prompting the sign EAT). He is also more willing to accept others touching his hands while signing or when sharing an activity together through mutual tactile attention or tactile modeling. Table 6.1 shows the identification cues of Manuel's communication

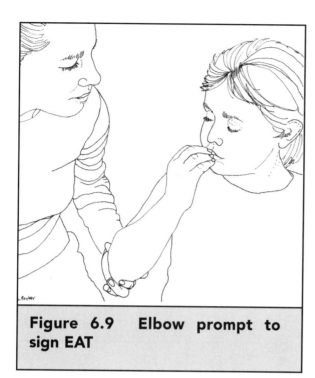

Figure 6.9   Elbow prompt to sign EAT

The communication cues and signs that are identified in the tables should be used within the context of ongoing conversations with Manuel.

SUMMARY

partners at home, Table 6.2 shows object cues and key word signs for home activities, and Table 6.3 shows the daily routine for feeding the dog. (See the Glossary at the back of this book for definitions of terms.)

Manual signs present an important option for communicative interactions with children who have deaf-blindness and other similar types of disabilities. Although normally a visual mode of communication, manual signs can be adapted to be produced tactilely and modified to be more tactilely salient for the child. Signs also can be modified to compensate for unique physical and cognitive needs of the child. Although using modified signs supports the unique needs of the child, however, the more signs that are modified, the harder they may be for conventional sign

TABLE 6.1 IDENTIFICATION CUES FOR MANUEL'S COMMUNICATION PARTNERS	
Communication partners	**Identification cue**
Foster mother (Carol)	Sign "C" on side of cheek
Foster father (Henry)	Sign "H" on forehead
Rosalee (daytime helper)	Feel braids
Bobby (evening helper)	Feel baseball cap
Tom (foster brother)	Feel rubber wrist band

Activity	Object cues and signs
TABLE 6.2 **OBJECT CUES AND SIGNS FOR SELECTED HOME ACTIVITIES**	
Mealtime	Cup (object cue) EAT (tactile or coactive signs)
Bath time	Bar of soap (object cue) BATH (sign on body)
Bedtime	Piece of foam (object cue) SLEEP (sign on body)
Feeding the dog	Cup to scoop food (object cue) DOG (tactile sign)
Walking the dog	Leash (object cue) DOG (tactile sign) WALK (tactile sign)
Helping with laundry	Laundry basket (object cue) HELP (tactile sign)
Buying a snack	Wallet with coins (object cues) BUY (tactile sign) CANDY (tactile and coactive sign)
Riding a horse	Piece of leather reins (object cue) HORSE (coactive and tactile signs)

Tactile strategies	Communication partner	Expectations of child	Response to child
TABLE 6.3 MANUEL AND HIS BROTHER FEED THE DOG			
Touch cue Object identification cue	Brother greets M. by giving him a "high five" and putting his wrist under M.'s hand so he can feel his rubber wrist band.	Recognize brother by greeting and identification cue.	Wait for M. to recognize his brother.
Tactile signing	Brother says and tactilely signs FEED DOG.	Recognize sign for DOG.	Give M. cup to scoop dog food and wheel him to kitchen area where dog food is kept
Tactile modeling Hand-under-hand guidance	Brother tactilely models how to scoop out a cup of dog food and put it into the bowl using hand-under-hand guidance.	Keep hands on brother's hands and on scoop during demonstration. Locate dog bowl. Scoop out another cup of dog food and put it in the bowl.	Wait for M. to scoop out dog food; praise M.'s efforts by patting him on the back.
Coactive signing	Brother calls dog "Archie" and helps M. sign DOG coactively.	Recognize sign and imitate it.	Dog comes to bowl and begins eating food; brother guides M. to pat dog's back.
Mutual tactile attention Tactile signing	Brother joins M. in rubbing dog's back.	Begin rubbing dog's back.	Repeat tactile sign for DOG.

users to understand. As with all modes of communication, adapted signs can be used for receptive communication, for expressive communication, or for both purposes. They also can be used in conjunction with other modes of communi- cation, such as touch cues, speech, and objects to make the interaction as clear as possible. Given the importance of effective communication for each child, the next chapter will provide additional information to support tactile interactions.

Chapter 7

Selecting Appropriate Tactile Strategies

The key to encouraging the effective use of tactile strategies with children who are blind and have additional disabilities lies in the initial selection of strategies and in their consistent and accurate use throughout the child's experiences. This chapter provides suggestions for selecting tactile strategies that are appropriate for an individual child and ways to address challenges in implementing these strategies.

The process of selecting the most appropriate tactile communication options for an individual child requires close collaboration between the child's family and educational program. The child's abilities as well as the child's limitations must be considered. What are the child's motor abilities? How does the child use his or her hands? Does the child have functional vision? How does the child react to being touched? How does the child communicate? The goal is to identify and to consistently use the most efficient means of receptive and expressive communication for the individual child. Table 7.1 provides a format for identifying the basic minimal skills that a child needs to make effective use of a tactile communication option.

CONSIDERATIONS FOR SELECTING STRATEGIES

Selecting tactile strategies that fit an individual child who is visually impaired and has additional disabilities requires thought and observation. The following considerations should guide the selection of individualized tactile strategies:

- Tactile strategies should reflect the child's abilities and preferences.

- Selected strategies should fit the child's abilities and needs.

- Selected strategies should be used consistently by all communication partners.

Strategies Should Reflect Abilities and Preferences

A child with a visual impairment and hearing loss may have additional diagnoses, such as cerebral palsy, hypotonia, or other medical needs. These multiple disabilities can create significant motor delays that may affect the ability to grasp, sit, stand, or move about independently. These children may experience tactile sensitivity or other challenges to using their hands and arms and may show strong dislike for certain textures (for example, things that are sticky or rough) or certain temperatures (for example, cold or warm). Family members and service providers should therefore consider the child's abilities and preferences when selecting a strategy. If a child is hyperreactive to certain types of tactile input, these types of materials or touch should be avoided. The child's occupational therapist should be consulted for suggestions of certain types of materials or activities and for how to encourage the child's tactile exploration (see Larrington, 2002).

Be sure to identify the child's tactile preferences and dislikes for the following:

- Liquids or drinks that are cold, warm, or at room temperature

- Surfaces that are smooth, rough, soft, or bumpy

TABLE 7.1 MINIMAL SKILLS FOR RECEPTIVE AND EXPRESSIVE TACTILE COMMUNICATION OPTIONS

Child's skills	Mutual tactile attention	Touch cue	Object cue	Hand-under-hand-guidance
Accepts tactile input	R/E	R/E	R/E	R
Makes minimal hand movements	R/E	E	R/E	
*Maintains contact	R/E		R/E	R
Opens hands				R
Conducts active exploration			E	

R = Minimal skill for the tactile option to be effective for receptive communication

E = Minimal skill for the tactile option to be effective for expressive communication

*Is able to maintain physical contact with an object or other person for a few seconds.

- Objects that vibrate, involve movement, or are still

- Materials that are wet, sticky, slimy, scratchy, or dry

In addition, the child's preferences for other sensory stimuli (for example, visual, auditory, movement, smell, or tastes) should be identified. A highly preferred activity may be used to support the child's handling of a material that is unfamiliar or

disliked. For example, if a child enjoys the movement and music of action songs, he or she may be encouraged to tactilely explore a material if this exploration is embedded within a song such as "This is the way we squish the mud, squish the mud, squish the mud."

Tactile strategies should engage the child's interaction and increase the probability of his or her response and participation. For example, Larry does not like his hands to be touched. Therefore, his

Hand-over-hand guidance	Tactile modeling	Coactive signing	Tactile signing
R	R	E	R/E
	R	E	R/E
R	R	E	R
R	R		R
	R		

communication partner should carefully observe to find out how, when, and where Larry accepts gentle and nonintrusive physical contact with his hand (that is, placing a hand beside Larry's hand or slightly under his fingers to establish mutual tactile attention). The communication partner may combine a highly preferred object with a nonpreferred object to increase the likelihood of the child making a choice. For instance, if a partner offers Marisa a choice between a vibrating ball and a stuffed animal, Marisa would most likely choose the vibrating ball because she enjoys that type of stimulation, and she does not like the texture of stuffed animals. However, even if a child's preference is known, partners should still offer a choice to increase communication opportunities for the child. Furthermore, a child's preference may change over time.

The following are some tips for using tactile strategies with a child:

1. Make sure that the child is in a symmetrical and secure position and provide adequate support.

2. Offer objects by placing them just beside and touching the child's fingers. If the child has limited hand control or keeps his or her hands in a fist, consult with the physical therapist regarding the best way to introduce an object to this child. Consider placing a desired toy on the child's chest, lap, or other part of the body if that placement encourages the child to reach and touch the object.

3. Offer objects within the child's reach and range of motion when the child has limited range of motion or motor abilities.

4. Provide adequate elbow support when needed to facilitate the child's action.

5. Provide physical adaptations to materials (for example, a Velcro strap, built-up handles, or a nonslip pad) to maximize the child's ability to grasp and manipulate objects.

Strategies Should Fit Abilities and Needs

A strategy is individually appropriate when it engages the child's participation and maximizes his or her understanding of the ongoing activity or interaction. Strategies should be adapted to meet the child's abilities and needs. For example, some children benefit from tactile signing, while others understand the information provided through object cues. See Table 7.2 for examples of strategies that are used effectively versus those that are used ineffectively.

TABLE 7.2 EFFECTIVE AND INEFFECTIVE TACTILE STRATEGIES

Effective strategies	Ineffective strategies
1. Tactilely signing DO YOU WANT A DRINK? under a child's hands if the child cooperates with placing his or her hands over the signer's hands	1. Producing visual signs beyond a child's visual field
2. Tactilely modeling YES for the child with your head and hands to show that you know he or she wants a drink	2. Making incomplete or inaccurate signs instead of accurately producing a sign (for example, coactively signing MORE by tapping fists together)
3. Placing a brush (object cue) in a child's hand for a few seconds before beginning to brush the child's hair so the child can anticipate what will happen	3. Signing a sequence of words rapidly to a child who has minimal understanding of signs
4. Establishing mutual tactile attention by gently touching a child's hands (without interrupting his or her attention) while engaged in an activity to let the child know that you see what he or she is doing	4. As an initial object cue, using a miniature object that the child does not perceive as representing the activity
5. Providing adequate elbow support (physical prompt) to maximize the child's ability to grasp and manipulate objects	5. Coactive signing when the child does not want his or her hands to be touched
6. Coactively signing FINISHED to mark the end of the activity with the child	

Strategies Should Be Used Consistently by All Communication Partners

Children with multiple disabilities are likely to have multiple service providers in addition to family members. Consistency will not only increase the child's understanding, expectations, and receptive communication, but it is also likely to support the child's expressive communication. An initial team meeting with service providers and family members is critical to promoting consistent use of cues and tactile strategies. In this way, everyone is involved in the selection of strategies and in the discussion of efficient ways to implement them. At first, a few strategies should be selected for the most frequent and preferred activities. Using ecological inventories (see Chapter 3) and creating a communication dictionary of the child's communication system (for example, touch and object cues, textured symbols, and adapted signs) serve as reminders of selected strategies. This communication dictionary should be reviewed and updated by team members regularly and will require a team member who is willing to take on this responsibility.

Although everyone who interacts with the child will undoubtedly have a unique style, these modes of interaction should not be so varied that a child cannot understand the message. This is the equivalent of each person speaking a different language. All team members should be aware of a standard procedure for interacting with the child and communicating a message so that the meaning is clear to the child, even though variables of voice and hands will inevitably be different. As discussed, it is most important to develop some shared system of communication, instructional strategies, and goals among family members and service providers. Regular communication may take place through meetings, logs, or online contacts. It is also important to collect and share data to identify what is effective and what needs to be changed in the child's educational program.

It is very difficult to always remember to do everything in a certain way, and there will be some natural differences in the use of tactile strategies between home and school and even among people in each of these places. For example, some family members may use "home" signs that they have invented, while others will use signs from ASL to communicate with the child. Over time, the child may learn to understand both types of signs. Similarly, at school some people may use a hand-over-hand prompt, while others may use object cues, and still others may use hand-under-hand techniques to perform the same task. Children can learn how to adapt to different expectations and varying communication methods; however, when a child requires support to develop communication, a consistent approach is likely to facilitate the learning process. Table 7.3 provides some examples of inconsistent communication methods.

OPPORTUNITIES FOR CONVERSATIONS

Children need multiple opportunities to communicate with many different people across a variety of situations. These opportunities support the child's social and

communication skills and expand his or her participation in ongoing activities. Many children who have multiple disabilities experience mainly adult-directed interactions with little opportunity for conversations or interactions with peers. Adults may interact with a child with multiple disabilities without expecting a response from the child. Most children are capable of some response—albeit one that is subtle and *initially* difficult to interpret.

TABLE 7.3 INCONSISTENT COMMUNICATION METHODS	
Action	**Communication methods**
Communicating "Let's go to the toilet"	• Adult 1 coactively signs TOILET with the child. • Adult 2 pats the child on his or her hip (touch cue).
Communicating "Lunch time"	• Adult 1 gives the child the selected object cue (for example, lunch ticket). • Adult 2 coactively signs LUNCH with the child.
Playing on the slide	• Adult 1 tactilely signs SLIDE under the child's hand. • Adult 2 signs SLIDE by stroking the child's arm (signs on body).
Encouraging independent eating	• Adult 1 uses hand-over-hand guidance to help the child. • Adult 2 prompts the child by providing support at the elbow.

Consider the following principles to guide the quality of interactions:

1. Expect a response from the child.

   - *Example:* You help the child to coactively sign DRINK when he or she appears to be ready for a drink. You wait 10 seconds for the child to respond. Providing the child with an opportunity to respond is critical for the child to learn that he or she is expected to communicate.

2. Select a strategy that will elicit an independent response from the child that is within his or her ability.

   - *Example:* Using object cues, you offer the child a choice between playing with musical instruments (preferred) or on the computer (disliked). You observe his or her body language and hand movements to interpret the response. Interpreting and responding to the child's preintentional behaviors—facial expressions, body movements, and other signals—will help shape the child's intentional communication efforts, such as use of gestures, vocalizations, and objects or words.

3. Encourage and support multiple conversational turns with the child within his or her ability.

   - *Example:* A child sits at the table for snack. You wait. The child searches table with hands, and you use an elbow prompt to encourage him or her to sign EAT. The child signs EAT and you tactilely sign YOU ARE HUNGRY. The child smiles, signs EAT again, you tactilely sign WANT COOKIE, and waits for the child to respond. The child signs COOKIE, so you tactilely sign YES EAT COOKIE and offer the plate of cookies. After the child takes and eats a cookie, you tactilely sign DELICIOUS.

4. Use the child's interest in an ongoing activity to guide your interactions.

   - *Example:* A peer is encouraged to use tactile signs with Marika, who is deaf-blind. After swinging together, the peer offers Marika a choice by tactilely signing WANT DRINK, BICYCLE, WHICH. Marika responds by signing DRINK, and her classmate helps her locate the water fountain. After both girls take a drink, the peer asks Marika if she wants to play at the water table by tactilely signing WATER PLAY. Marika signs YES. Her friend guides her to the water table, and together they play with the materials there.

PROBLEM SOLVING

At times, children may be unresponsive, and the usual recommended strategies do not seem to work. A child may not demonstrate the desired responses for several reasons. To figure out the best approach to this situation, the following strategies are suggested:

- Gather information.

- Determine which modes of sensory input provide the most efficient information.

- Help the child overcome resistance to touching items and using his or her hands.

Gather Information

Before a solution can be determined, information is needed about the reason for the child's reluctance to interact or participate. All behaviors communicate, so it is critical to determine what the child is trying to say by his or her refusal to participate (O'Neill et al., 1997; Sigafoos, 2000). Functional

analysis—the systematic observation of a child's clearly defined behavior across different settings, activities, and people—can help identify the variables controlling and maintaining the behavior. Observation entails the documentation of potential antecedents of the behavior (what happened before) as well as consequences of the behavior (what actually happened after).

Information gathering also involves interviewing significant others who may be able to describe what preceding events could have had an impact on the observed behavior, when the behavior is most likely to occur, and what the behavior is likely to mean for the child. Once all information is gathered about the child's behavior, an initial analysis is done to develop a hypothesis about the intent of the child's behavior. The hypothesis, in turn, leads to an intervention strategy designed to help support the child's communication skills (see O'Neill, et al., 1997). The following questions highlight the relation of functional analysis to potentially resistive communication behavior:

- When is the child most likely to resist interactions?

- What is happening during these times?

- How is the interaction taking place (for example, what physical strategies are being used)?

- What are the expectations?

- What materials are being used?

- Is the context motivating?

The goal of the information-gathering process is to determine what the child is trying to communicate so family members and service providers can make accommodations and change the quality of the interaction. This helps demonstrate respect for the child and establish a trusting relationship. Once this information has been obtained, a hypothesis can be generated about the function that the behavior serves for the child. For instance, the child may be trying to avoid something disliked, obtain something else that is desired but not offered, or obtain attention. Once the message or messages being conveyed by the child are clear, systematic intervention can be implemented to help the child have these needs met while also teaching more appropriate ways to express such needs.

For example, 4-year-old Roger, who is deaf-blind, appeared to be somewhat resistant to interaction with his two older brothers. When they tried to engage him in a simple game like tossing a soft Nerf ball or playing with sofa pillows, Roger would scream and pull away from them, wildly flapping his arms and hands. Repeated observation of this behavior revealed that it occurred mainly with his siblings and usually before he had gone to the bathroom and before he had eaten breakfast, lunch, dinner, or a snack. Furthermore, the behavior appeared to be most intense when Roger's mother was not around.

His brothers tended to begin playing with him rather suddenly by thrusting items into his face or hands and manipulating his hands and arms to get him to play with them. Roger was not given time to understand the expectations or "rules" of the game. His mother felt that in these situations, Roger was startled, unable to grasp his brothers' intentions or recognize materials, and felt insecure and anxious, especially when she was not around. She also hypothesized that he was not ready to play until he had been to the bathroom and had something to eat. With this information, the team was able to determine the rationale for Roger's "resistant behavior" and to develop a plan that would better fit Roger's needs. Roger's brothers and other peers were asked to respect Roger's communicative behaviors that indicated "no" and to wait until he was comfortable after meeting his basic needs before trying to engage him in play. Moreover, they needed to learn how to introduce the game and play materials slowly, giving Roger time to get ready for the interaction and building repetitive actions so that Roger could develop an understanding of a predictable sequence of actions. Further, his brothers needed to observe and respond to Roger's communicative behaviors that indicated when he wanted to continue to play and when he had had enough.

Determine the Most Efficient Sensory Input Modes

Because the child's ability to understand information is likely to vary from situation to situation, it is important to be flexible and try different approaches. Different strategies may be needed depending on the situation; the demands of the task; the child's ability level, motivation, and attention; and environmental factors such as lighting and background noise. For some situations, the use of a particular object cue (for example, a favorite toy) will provide the necessary information for the child to understand what is expected. At other times, an object cue may not make sense to the child; however, the sound of the object (for example, an electric keyboard) and physical support for the child to move to the vibrations might be more effective in communicating the message.

Sometimes a child's limited physical ability to thoroughly explore and identify items tactilely requires the use of other modes of input. For example, Jay has extreme difficulty in reaching out to feel items and will not explore what is directly in front of him. Instead, his teacher brings a cup of dried rice from the rice table to him so he can feel the rice and recognize that playing at the rice table is the next activity. However, at other times, small items can be placed close by for him to explore. He needs to know that the item is in front of him and he needs plenty of time to explore the item on his own without being forced to do so. Knowing that another person is interacting with the item that is close to him without the demand for him to touch the item can help to establish a trusting situation and make him more inclined to interact with the item on his own.

Help Overcome Resistance to Touch and Hand Use

Sometimes children will refuse to touch items and will actively clench their fists and pull their hands away from items that have been presented. These types of refusals can occur for a variety of reasons. If the child is saying "no" through his or her body movements and facial expressions, caregivers must respect this communication and alter the situation so that the child will be more likely to participate. Consider the following questions:

- Are there other things that the child will touch and wants to engage? Is this an option?

- Has a trusting relationship been established with the child so that he or she can feel comfortable exploring items?

- Are the child's hands respected as sense organs that gather information through touch?

Take care that the child is comfortable using his or her hands without fear of being forced to touch unwanted or aversive objects. Using mutual tactile attention by focusing on a child's action and gently following his or her lead helps the child to understand that someone is paying attention to his or her action. Encouraging children to engage in mutual tactile attention by touching items with another person is also important so that they become comfortable with participating in interactions. Children who can see spend considerable time watching their family members and others, and these experiences motivate them to try what they see based on other people's reactions. Without vision, children must rely on tactile information, and the process of learning through touch takes much more time than learning through vision, so caregivers must ensure that children who learn by touch are provided with sufficient time, opportunities, and supports.

FREQUENTLY ASKED QUESTIONS

This selection of frequently asked questions is based on the questions from and discussions with families and service providers who participated in Project SALUTE activities and workshops. The answers are drawn from the review of the literature and from the clinical judgment and experiences of service providers and professionals who have worked with children who have significant and multiple disabilities. The suggestions offered in the responses will need to be tailored to the needs and abilities of each individual child who demonstrates the challenge described in a particular question.

Sensory Input

Q. How do I determine which types of sensory input (visual, auditory, tactile) provide the most useful information to a child who is nonverbal and has low vision and other disabilities?

Carefully observe the child's response to various sensory input in different situations to see how the child responds and what he or she seems to understand. Even when a child has some vision and hearing, he or she may benefit from tactile input at specific times (for example, if the environment is dark or noisy). Some children's ability to use vision may vary according to their level of alertness and health and the context. (This is frequently true, for example, for children with cortical visual impairment, a condition in which visual impairment is caused by damage to the brain, while the eye is normal.) A child may need to use touch to help confirm or clarify what he or she sees. It is helpful to collect data on the child's responses to different modes of sensory input in various situations. Also, functional vision and hearing assessments should be used to determine how the child is using these senses.

Q. Should I use tactile strategies when the child has some vision?

There are many reasons why the use of tactile strategies may benefit a child with multiple disabilities. All children learn through a combination of input from their senses. When children have multiple disabilities and subtle responses to visual stimuli, it may be difficult to determine whether the child has a clear understanding of what is being presented or communicated through visual means. Because it is very concrete, tactile information will supplement visual input or clarify other sensory input.

Q. Will the use of tactile strategies interfere with a child's learning to use his or her vision?

In our experience, the use of tactile strategies will not inhibit or prevent a child from learning to use his or her vision. Appropriate modifications to materials and the environment (for example, positioning, color, contrast, and lighting) also need to be made to encourage the child's use of functional vision. In fact, increased active participation in interactions and activities resulting from the use of tactile strategies should also motivate a child to learn to look. Some children with cortical visual impairment have difficulty looking at and reaching for or manipulating an object at the same time. They may look, then look away, and reach or tactilely examine the object. It is important for family members and service providers to

agree on the strategies they will use with a child—for example, to first present objects visually to a child, and then, after several seconds, provide an opportunity for the child to touch and handle the object. In this way, what the child feels will confirm or clarify what he or she sees.

Tactile Strategies

Q. Is there a sequence for beginning to use tactile strategies with a young child?

There is no single sequence for using tactile strategies that fits every child who has multiple disabilities. Each situation is different, and tactile strategies need to be selected accordingly. Begin establishing interaction and supporting the child's communication development with mutual tactile attention. As discussed, every child needs both a means to receive communication and a way to express himself or herself. Begin by carefully observing the child in familiar activities with preferred people. What are the features of preferred objects? What situations seem to be the most motivating for the child? Note how the child uses the sense of touch to explore and interact with others and how he or she responds to tactile input from others.

Q. How do we decide which tactile communication strategies (coactive signs, signs on body, tactile signs, touch cues, object cues, or textured symbols) to use with a child who is deaf-blind?

First, identify the child's receptive and expressive communication behaviors. Next, consider the child's motor and cognitive abilities. Use techniques that the child will easily understand so he or she will experience immediate pleasure and reinforcement for effort during interactions. If there is little or no response from the child, try a strategy that provides more concrete information (for example, use whole objects that are familiar to the child). Be sure that any strategy is integrated in natural, respectful, and enjoyable conversations that involve turn-taking and shared attention. Over time, a child may progress to more abstract and complex communication modes.

Q. How do we determine whether to use a textured symbol or an object cue?

Object cues are easily understood because of their obvious relationship to their referents (for example, a cup to represent "drink"). When it is difficult or inconvenient to use an object cue (for example, to represent "let's go outside and play on the lawn"), then a more abstract communication mode, such as a textured symbol, may be needed. (See the discussions of object cues and textured symbols in Chapter 5.) What an object cue or textured symbol represents must be made immediately apparent to a child (that is, by giving the child the item, beginning an activity, or going to the place) so he or she will understand its meaning.

Q. What should I do to help the child understand what the textured symbols or object cues mean?

The key to helping a child understand the meaning of any communication cue or symbol is to *link it closely* to its referent—through mutual tactile attention within conversations, for example—and to use it *consistently* within meaningful activities in a variety of settings. The child needs to learn that a particular textured card or object stands for a particular activity or object. When the child touches the textured card or object, he or she must receive or experience the referent immediately.

Q. How can a child who is blind differentiate between a touch cue and a sign made on his or her body?

Initially, the child may perceive the sign made on his or her body as a touch cue having a very fixed meaning within a specific context. For example, if the signer places his or her hand on the child's mouth to sign EAT, the child will feel the placement of the touch on his or her mouth and not perceive the flat "O" hand shape that is a feature of EAT. Through consistent exposure to the sign (that is, by encouraging the child to feel the signer's hands and by using coactive and tactile signs) and its referents (objects, people, or activities), he or she may gradually recognize that a sign produced on his or her body has the same meaning when it is produced coactively or signed tactilely in different situations.

Q. I confuse coactive signing and tactile signing. How are they different?

Tactile signing is a means of receptive communication. The child tactilely perceives or reads the signs by keeping his or her hand over the signer's hand. Coactive signing is used for instructional purposes, to teach a child how to produce a new sign in the appropriate situation or to help a child produce signs to convey a message that he or she wants to express. Use tactile signing when you want to send the child a message and coactive signing when the child wants to communicate something. Just as listening precedes speaking in children who can see and hear, understanding tactile signs (receptive language) precedes the production of signs (expressive language) by children who have a hearing loss and no vision.

Q. How can I develop a concrete way to let a child know that he or she has completed a particular activity, rather than just by signing FINISHED?

Often children who are blind and nonverbal may not know how long an activity will last or understand our expectations for a particular task. They may be quite startled by a sign for FINISH that seems to come out of nowhere. It is important to make the message and expectation very concrete and easy to understand. One simple way is to tell the child how many times he or she is expected to do a task and make that expectation apparent from the materials that are available. For example, in a play activity involving blocks and a container, put out five blocks for the child and, using key tactile signs, say "PUT BLOCKS IN BUCKET, 1, 2, 3, 4, 5, FINISH." Similarly, when it's time to clean up, you can specify how many things the child needs to locate and put away and the names of those things. For example, "Jimmy, find the car and the hat and put them away." This is helpful if the child cannot see whether or not the whole area is cleaned up. Similarly, you can let the child know that there are "five more minutes of playtime." Such an introduction to number and time concepts within everyday activities will build on the child's early literacy skills. At music or circle time, provide a tray or container with objects or other tactile representations of songs and activities so the child can make a choice and also learn that when the tray is empty the activity will end. Again, telling the child, "one more song and then we are finished," is also important. A modified timer may also be useful if the child can hear the buzzer or bell.

Challenges

Q. What can I do if a child is tactilely defensive and hates to touch things?

First of all, do not force the child to touch and handle the things that he or she rejects. Very often, the term "tactilely defensive" is misused by service providers to label a child who does not want to touch or handle certain materials. Tactile defensiveness is a specific type of sensory defensiveness—hypersensitivity to touch. Some children with disabilities may avoid touching certain materials that are novel, uninteresting, or frightening. They may overreact to someone touching if they find this type of interaction threatening or are not prepared for the interaction. It is most important to consult with an occupational therapist that has expertise in sensory integration (the organization and processing of sensory information). He or she will have specific procedures for identifying whether a child's responses are indicative of tactile defensiveness, some other sensory defensiveness, or hyperresponsiveness to certain sensory stimuli. If the occupational therapist determines that the child has a sensory modulation dysfunction—that is, impaired ability to manage reactions to sensory input—then he or she will recommend certain activities to address this neurologically based problem. If the child's reluctance to touch and handle certain materials is based on unpleasant experiences, take time to develop a trusting relationship, make your hands quietly available to the child, and use mutual tactile attention, tactile modeling, and hand-under-hand guidance to gradually offer opportunities to touch, explore, and handle preferred objects without forcing the child to do so. Provide anticipatory cues and expand the child's communication and understanding of activities.

Q. How can I encourage service providers to be more consistent in the use of selected tactile strategies for a particular child?

Children who have multiple disabilities are likely to interact with many different service providers during their school programs. It will be very confusing for the child if each person uses a different method of communication and has conflicting expectations. The child's communication options should be noted in the IFSP or IEP. It is very important to have a team meeting with family members and service providers who interact most frequently with the child to identify and agree on tactile strategies that will be used consistently. Practicing selected strategies and viewing videos of the child's interactions are very helpful procedures. Once strategies are selected and agreed upon, methods for sharing information, documenting practice, and planning for follow-up are needed. Post written guidelines for the use of cues and signs in easily accessible places. Also, use data collection sheets, communication notes, or e-mail to document practice and share information. Short, regularly scheduled meetings facilitate opportunities for data analysis, evaluation of current strategies, and agreements on any changes that need to be made.

Q. When interacting with my child, I have realized that I pay more attention to his facial expression and body movements than his hands. How can I become more aware of my child's hands to engage in tactile conversations?

First, become more aware of how you use your own hands when interacting with your child. Use the self-awareness questions in Chapter 1 to think about your own body language. Next, carefully observe your child's hands while he or she is interacting with objects and people. Become familiar with his or her hand movements. Practice focusing on the child's hands as well as his or her facial expressions and body movements during interactions. Try closing your eyes during touch conversations between your hands and the child's hands. This will help you become aware of how your hands receive tactile information from your child.

Q. What should I do if a child persists in putting objects in his or her mouth rather than touching them with his or her hands?

Safety is a priority, so children must not be allowed to put small objects or other health hazards in their mouths. Young children without disabilities vary in the age at which they no longer put things in their mouths (Juberg, Alfano, Coughlin & Thompson, 2001), but this mouthing behavior does not inhibit their hand use. Children who are blind may use mouthing as a way to maintain contact with and obtain information about an object. If so, objects should be washed for hygienic purposes. Children usually decrease their mouthing of objects as they

increase their hand use. Play activities that involve throwing in appropriate situations—for example, throwing beanbags onto a big drum—may promote outward hand movements that will help separate the child's hand from his or her mouth. If mouthing is a concern, professionals of relevant disciplines, such as occupational therapy, visual impairment, or nursing, should develop a working hypothesis about the function of the mouthing behavior, using the following types of questions: What sorts of objects are mouthed? Does the child seem to discriminate between certain sizes, shapes, or textures through mouthing? How does the child use his or her hands? When and how does he or she touch and handle objects? Will the child touch and handle objects if something is in his or her mouth (for example, a pacifier for a toddler)? Through a comprehensive interdisciplinary analysis, an appropriate approach can be developed to encourage the child's manual exploration.

Q. What can I do if a child rejects my efforts to interact with him or her and seems more interested in engaging in self-stimulatory behaviors (for example, patting self or objects)?

Remember that a child needs to "see" an activity before he or she will want to participate. Concentrate on providing opportunities for the child to touch your hands and objects without the expectation that he or she participate in a certain way. Spend time just making your hands available to the child and see what he or she does. Have fun making "conversations with hands" by imitating the child's hand movements in a gentle and playful way. It takes time to establish a relationship and to develop an understanding of the child's experience and perspective. Carefully observe the child's actions and identify when you might join in them. For example, if a child persists in patting an object, you could gently place your hand beside his or her hand and imitate the patting action, thus communicating, "I see what you are doing. Let's pat together" (mutual tactile attention). Once the child accepts your imitative tactile interaction, try to introduce another activity involving a different hand movement (for example, varying the tapping rhythm) or object (for example, introducing a drum). This will provide a basis for developing other kinds of social games and interactions.

Q. My child dislikes having his hands touched or manipulated. How can we interact with him in a more acceptable way?

Do not manipulate your child's hands or force him to touch something that he resists. Consult with an occupational therapist regarding the child's hand use and responses to tactile input and obtain suggestions. Use tactile strategies that allow the child to maintain control over his own hands (see the discussions on mutual tactile attention, hand-under-hand, and hierarchy of prompts in Chapters 3 and 4).

Create playful interactions involving hand games or finger plays that you both enjoy (for example, "pat-a-cake" for a young child and "high fives" for an older one), and follow the child's lead by imitating his manual actions (for example, clapping hands, tapping a tambourine, or playing a keyboard).

Q. My child is totally blind and has some hearing as well as poor muscle strength (very low tone). He doesn't like to manipulate or explore objects. I have to manipulate his hands to help him with everything. How can I help my child participate without continuously moving his hands?

Discuss your concern with your child's teacher and physical or occupational therapist to determine the best way to help your child. Depending on your child's motor ability, they may suggest some simple adaptations to materials (for example, Velcro or built-up handles on objects to help your child grasp them), ways to increase the child's attention (for example, by tactile kinesthetic play), as well as ways to gradually decrease his dependence on your total physical assistance. Begin with activities that your child enjoys so that he is motivated to participate. Instead of using hand-over-hand guidance, try supporting him at the wrist or elbow to see how he responds to those physical prompts. See how he responds to hand-under-hand guidance when you introduce your hand under his. Will he keep his hand on top of yours if you touch his hand with your finger?

Q. My child is blind and has severe cerebral palsy. He has very limited hand and arm movement and tends to keep his hands in fists. What kind of tactile strategies can I use?

Ask to meet with your child's educational team to discuss your questions. The physical or occupational therapist can explain your child's motor abilities and optimal positioning needs and may suggest ways to help decrease your child's tone to help him open his hands. The speech and language therapist and teacher will have suggestions about adaptive switches or other communication devices to support your child's communication. Together you can determine what tactile strategies to try first and how your child uses and responds to tactile information and interactions.

Q. How do you know what a child is learning (for example, when he or she understands language/communication input)? How do you determine the next step?

Evaluating whether an instructional strategy is effective for a particular child is a priority in teaching all children who have disabilities. Otherwise, we would not be providing the most appropriate educational opportunities. It's a challenge to determine what a child is learning if the child has significant and multiple disabilities that influence his or her behaviors. The child's responses may be extremely

subtle or unusual. Careful observation, systematic interaction, data collection, and analysis of the child's behaviors are essential in determining what a child is learning. How does the child respond to a "delay" or "interruption" of a very predictable sequence in an activity? How does the child react when he or she is given the object cue for a certain activity? Videotape an interaction or routine when the child is first learning about it, and then do so again later on when he or she has become more familiar with the activity. Comparing the child's behaviors on these tapes may be helpful in identifying subtle changes in his or her quality of responses.

Q. How can I encourage other children to use tactile strategies with a child who is deaf-blind?

It is very important to encourage interactions with peers because most children like and learn from their peers. Moreover, many children with significant disabilities have limited opportunities to interact with other children unless adults provide sufficient support. Similarly, children without disabilities need to learn how to interact effectively with a child who is deaf-blind. You can use your own interactions as a model. Help children follow the interest and lead of the child who is deaf-blind rather than manipulating his or her hands. Teach them how to adapt signs appropriately for the individual child who is deaf-blind, and show them simple strategies such as offering an object under or to the side of the child's hand rather than physically moving his or her hand to the object. Discuss the importance of waiting for the child to respond by allowing enough time. Help children practice tactile strategies with each other or an adult. Encourage them to interpret the behavioral responses of the child who is deaf-blind and respond appropriately.

SUMMARY

This chapter has addressed how to select the specific tactile strategies that are appropriate for an individual child. Through responses to questions asked by both family members and service providers, it has also addressed specific challenges that may be encountered in supporting the development of a child who is visually impaired and has other significant disabilities.

It is equally important to encourage the development of academic skills specifically related to a formal education. The next chapter discusses specific strategies that focus on the development of literacy skills for children who are blind and have significant multiple disabilities. Literacy skills—at any level—open doors to increased learning opportunities for children. Furthermore, literacy learning can be made accessible to all children regardless of ability level.

Chapter 8

Encouraging Emergent Literacy

Communication skills lay the foundation for early literacy skills by increasing a child's awareness and understanding of language, basic concepts, and learning in general. Although the current emphasis on literacy for all children has been promoted by statewide education standards and the No Child Left Behind Act (NCLB, 2002), literacy for children who are visually impaired and have additional disabilities has long been a concern for educators and families alike. Children with such multiple disabilities often have limited access to the typical life experiences that form the foundation for later literacy learning. Literacy develops as the child naturally experiences daily activities, situations, and objects, and sees and hears language as it takes on a written form. As Wormsley (1997) has noted, "The process of becoming familiar with written language is generally known as *emergent literacy*—the term refers to the time during which literacy is 'emerging' in the child" (p. 17). For most children, familiarity with written language begins with an early exposure to print in books, on toys, on containers of food, and other everyday experiences that occur in the first years of life.

USING TACTILE BOOKS AND BOXES

Children who are blind, have additional disabilities, and do not have symbolic language need access to early literacy experiences by "reading" tactile representations of real life experiences. Such tactile strategies can play a pivotal role in encouraging emergent literacy in the child with severe multiple disabilities regardless of the child's age. For example, object schedules can be used as an introduction to literacy. The child "reads" the schedule for the day by identifying the objects and the activities they represent. Tactile books, journals, scrapbooks, or boxes should also be created by using tactile remnants, symbols, or reminders of activities that the child experiences. Children's preferences and interests should be used as a basis for the initial experiences that will be tactilely represented. In addition, adults need to point out the salient features of the representations to the child. The representative tactile symbol should be paired with the experience consistently as it occurs, so that its meaning will be clear in literacy activities.

Each page of a tactile book can hold one tactile remnant with a story line added in print, braille, or both. To help the reader use signs to support communication with the child who is deaf-blind, pictures of the signs for key words may be placed on each page as shown in the book about going camping in Figure 8.1. The picture of key signs (for example, TREE, TENT) may serve as a reminder to the adult or peer to produce the signs and to tactilely show them to the child as they read the book together. In this way, the child who is deaf-blind can feel the braille and the representation object and learn to associate the item with the sign.

A tactile book about going to the beach might have a key on one page to recall going in the car and driving to the beach, some sand on another page to represent walking or playing in the sand, some small shells on another page to indicate collecting shells, and so on. In this way, the child can recall events while learning about books, turning pages, identifying information (reading) on each page, and sharing experiences with others. Tactile books require materials that must be adapted and individualized for each child, but they are well worth the time and effort. They make it possible for all children to have literacy experiences (Downing, 2005b, Lewis & Tolla, 2003). The following are some examples of the use of tactile books:

- José's sixth grade class trip to an amusement park is recreated tactilely using items from the trip (for example, part of the popcorn box, the wristband that got him onto rides, a straw for the drink that was purchased, or a small souvenir) in the story or scrapbook box. José's grandfather discusses the event while encouraging him to manipulate each object. Each item is labeled in braille and print with an age-appropriate comment, such as, "Hey, look at what I got at Disneyland."

- Fung's day is created tactilely in a book format. An item or part of an item is attached to each page of the book with a phrase or sentence written beneath the item in both braille and print. With her mother and sister, Fung shares her day through mutual tactile attention by touching items on each page and then turning the page. Her mother or sister reads the phrases as Fung tactilely examines the item. (Figure 8.2 shows mutual tactile attention to a book.)

- Brandon, a kindergartner, is visually impaired with additional disabilities and without functional vision. Rather than pictures of items whose names begin with the letters of the alphabet, his ABC box contains objects or parts of objects that represent selected words (similar objects may also be displayed in a

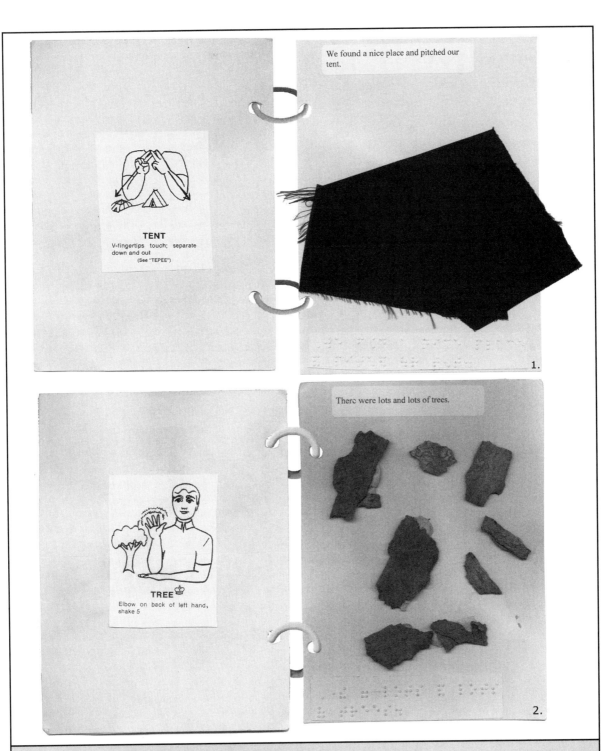

We found a nice place and pitched our tent.

TENT
V-fingertips touch; separate down and out
(See "TEPEE")

1.

There were lots and lots of trees.

TREE ♔
Elbow on back of left hand, shake 5

2.

Figure 8.1 Pages from a tactile book: Going camping

Signing Exact English illustrations supplied by Modern Signs Press, Inc.

book). For example, Brandon has objects to represent A for apple, B for balloon, and C for cookie. He can handle and explore these meaningful objects that he experiences in everyday life.

- Sally, a first grader, reads a book from the American Printing House for the Blind about pockets and what are in them by turning each page of the book to feel the pocket and look inside each one. She feels the braille words while a peer reads

the print. Tactile signs for each item are also provided to Sally.

- Ali's fourth grade class is reading *Harry Potter and the Sorcerer's Stone* by J. K. Rowling. They role-play riding a broom, making things disappear by magic, and wearing "wizard" hats. Ali has access to all these items as well, and he engages in the role-play with his classmates. His tactile book has pieces of the actual items on individual pages. His classmates also provide tactile signs

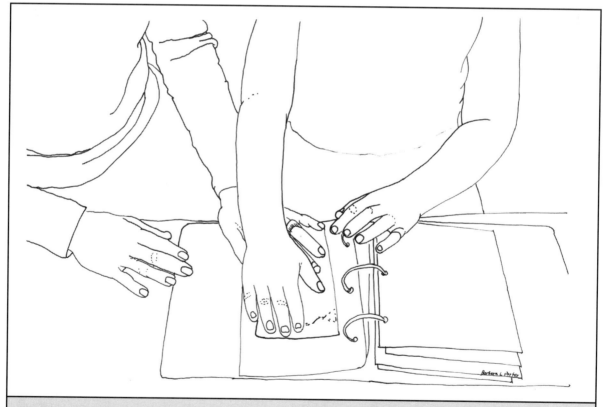

Figure 8.2 Mutual tactile attention: Reading a tactile book

for HAT, WAND, and BROOM as they read the adapted story line that they developed.

PROMOTING LITERACY

Children who are blind and have additional disabilities need to be exposed to braille in consistent and meaningful ways. There are commercially available materials, such as TACK-TILES (see the Resources section), to help children who are blind and have additional disabilities learn to read braille. Some professionals recommend uncontracted braille (which has no contractions and a one-to-one correspondence with written English) for children who are blind and have multiple disabilities. Over time, some children may learn to discriminate and recognize braille labels of favorite items, names, and words in tactile books and other words in braille (Wormsley, 2004).

The following are some suggestions for promoting English literacy experiences:

1. Provide language-rich activities, materials, and environments to support a child's experiences with literacy. These include playing together, describing objects, discussing events, and supporting the child's access to language, conversations, stories, and books.

2. As appropriate, use varied intonation, gestures, signs, objects, and tactile items to engage the child in a conversation or story.

3. Build on real experiences that the child enjoys as a beginning point for literacy experiences by referring to tactile items associated with these experiences. These tactile items should be organized in a story or scrapbook box or book so that the child can refer to events and "reread" these stories. For example, to recreate the experience of going horseback riding with the family, various items such as straw, alfalfa, horse hair, horse food pellets, and leather strips (reins) can be collected and glued on paper with a few sentences in print and braille to create a story for others to read to the child.

4. Provide opportunities for children to feel other people making use of these tactile books or scrapbook boxes. That is, let the child explore another person's hands and what is tactilely represented on each page while another person is reading the book.

5. Expose the child to braille in a similar manner to the way young sighted children are exposed to print—for example, on labels. The child should feel the braille even though he or she may not be able to read this abstract symbol system. Through repeated and consistent

exposures, the child will assign meaning to the braille dots.

6. Read familiar, interesting, and relevant books repeatedly with the child so he or she can feel the rhythm. For example, as the adult reads the story, he or she taps out the rhythm and repetition of the spoken words. The child can also place his or her hands on the adult's throat to feel the rhythm of the spoken words. Try reading stories that have repetitive lines (like, "Brown bear, brown bear, what do you see?") or rhyming lines (as in Dr. Seuss books) that have a clear rhythm and beat that the child can begin to anticipate over time.

7. Ask the child to "read" a favorite book to you by touching tactile items in sequence and using gestures or other means of communication.

8. Provide opportunities for interaction. Pause during the story and wait for the child to feel tactile items and the braille and to comment or anticipate what happens next. Allow the child to hold the book, turn the pages, and manipulate tactile features. If needed, add tabs to the pages to make them easier for the child to turn.

9. Have the child participate in the creation of tactile books and displays using items that represent favorite activities or experiences.

10. Whenever possible, help the child make connections between these experience stories and current or upcoming events. For example, before going out on a similar activity, reintroduce the book and read with the child to prepare him or her for the upcoming activity. Also, when relatives or friends come over, the child can be encouraged to read this experimental book with them and retell the activity once again.

11. Include individualized tactile books in a child's portfolio that will follow the child from grade to grade, and inform future teachers of how the child accesses literacy activities.

12. As the child gains greater understanding of different literacy experiences, more and more abstract methods of representation can be used. Braille and print should always be included in a tactile book to outline the story, even though the child may not be able to understand these abstract forms. The inclusion of sentences in braille and print ensures repetition and consistent language input when the story is being read to the child. Further, the child may become familiar with some words in braille (if he or she is encouraged to feel the braille dots) or print (if he or she has sufficient vision) through repeated exposure. Every effort should

be made to fade more concrete forms of representation (for example, whole objects) to more abstract forms (for example, small parts of objects). Some children who have low vision may learn to make the connection between objects and their pictorial representations. Concrete objects that represent activities that are highly motivating and familiar may be replaced with more abstract representations more quickly than others (for example, replacing the empty McDonald's French fries package with a colorful picture of fries). Other representations that are less motivating may need to remain concrete for the child to understand them.

13. The use of jumbo braille cells for reading may be helpful for some children; using muffin tins with golf balls may be helpful for younger children if they can later transfer these skills to regular-size braille.

14. Let children experiment and play with braillewriters as a form of written self-expression. This might be considered "doodling" in braille.

SUMMARY

Learning literacy skills is important for all children, whether or not they have acquired an abstract language system. Family members and school personnel will need to create meaningful tactile representations of events and interests to serve as literacy materials for children who do not read in a more conventional manner. Children can be encouraged to feel the representative items and recall the event or experience. In this manner, children begin to learn basic skills to further literacy skills development. Tactile books also provide a glimpse into the child's personality by revealing the types of activities that he or she likes, by showing how the child "reads" the book, and by providing opportunities for interaction with peers. Efforts to support emergent literacy and the development of literacy skills in children are among the most worthwhile of investments, helping to lay the foundation for a child's ongoing growth and development.

References

Aitken, S., Buultjens, M., Clark, C., Eyre, J. T., & Pease, L. (2000). *Teaching children who are deafblind: Contact, communication and learning.* London: David Fulton Publishers.

Alsop, L. (Ed.) (2002). *Understanding deafblindness: Issues, perspectives, and strategies* (Vols. 1 & 2). Logan, UT: SKI-HI Institute, HOPE.

Barraga, N. C. (1986). Sensory perceptual development. In G.T. Scholl (Ed.), *Foundations of education for blind and visually impaired children and youth: Theory and practice* (pp. 83–98). New York: AFB Press.

Barraga, N. C., & Erin, J. (1992). *Visual handicaps and learning* (3rd ed.). Austin, TX: PRO-ED.

Best, A., & Boothroyd, E. (Eds.) (1998, June). *Objects of reference: Report of the exploratory meeting.* Shrewsbury, Shropshire, UK: Condover Hall School, Royal National Institute for the Blind.

Beukelman, D. R., & Mirenda, P. (1998). *Augmentative and alternative communication: Management of severe communication disorders in children and adults* (2nd ed.). Baltimore: Paul H. Brookes.

Blackwell, P. L. (2000). The influence of touch on child development: Implications for intervention. *Infants and Young Children, 13*(1), 25–39.

Blaha, R. (2002). *Calendars for students with multiple disabilities including deafblindness.* Austin: Texas School for the Blind and Visually Impaired.

Blaha, R., & Carlson, B. (1996). Issues regarding the assessment of vision loss in regard to sign language and finger spelling for the student with deaf-blindness. *SEE/HEAR.* Retrieved August 10, 2001, from http://www.tsbvi.edu/Outreach/seehear/archive/sign.html

Blissymbolics Communication Institute. (1984). *Picture your Blisssymbols instructional manual.* Toronto: Author.

Bradley-Johnson, S., Johnson, C. M., Swanson, J., & Jackson, A. (2004). Exploratory behavior: A comparison of infants who are congenitally blind and infants who are sighted. *Journal of Visual Impairment & Blindness, 98,* 496–502.

Bushnell, E. W., & Boudreau, J. P. (1991). The development of haptic perception during infancy. In M. A. Heller & W. Schiff (Eds.), *The psychology of touch* (pp. 139–161). Hillsdale, NJ: Lawrence Erlbaum Associates.

Catherwood, D., Drew, L., Hein, B., & Grainger, H. (1998). Haptic recognition in two infants with low vision assessed by a familiarization procedure. *Journal of Visual Impairment & Blindness, 92,* 212–215.

Chen, D. (1995). The beginnings of communication: Early childhood. In K. M. Huebner, J. G. Prickett, T. R. Welch, & E. Joffee (Eds.), *Hand in hand: Essentials of communication and orientation and mobility for your students who are deaf-blind* (pp. 185–218). New York: AFB Press.

Chen, D. (1999). Beginning communication with infants. In D. Chen (Ed.), *Essential elements in early intervention. Visual impairments and multiple disabilities* (pp. 337–377). New York: AFB Press.

Chen, D., Downing, J., & Rodriguez-Gil, G. (2000). Tactile learning strategies for children who are deaf-blind: Concerns and considerations from Project SALUTE. *DeafBlind Perspectives, 8*(1), 1–6.

Dote-Kwan, J., & Chen, D. (1999). Developing meaningful interventions. In D. Chen (Ed.), *Essential elements in early intervention: Visual impairments and multiple disabilities* (pp. 287–336). New York: AFB Press.

Downing, J. E. (2003). Accommodating motor and sensory impairments in inclusive settings. In D. L. Ryndak & S. Alper (Eds.), *Curriculum and instruction for students with significant disabilities in inclusive settings* (2nd ed., pp. 411–429). Boston: Allyn and Bacon.

Downing, J. E. (2005a). *Teaching communication skills to students with severe disabilities* (2nd ed.). Baltimore: Paul H. Brookes.

Downing, J. E. (2005b). *Teaching literacy for students with significant disabilities: Strategies for inclusive K–12 classrooms.* Thousand Oaks, CA: Corwin Press.

Downing, J. E., & Chen, D. (2003). Tactile strategies: Interacting with students who are blind and have severe disabilities. *TEACHING Exceptional Children, 36*(2), 56–61.

Downing, J. E., & Peckham-Hardin, K. (2001). Daily schedules: A helpful learning tool. *Teaching Exceptional Children, 33*(3), 62–68.

Dresser, N. (1996). *Multicultural manners. New rules of etiquette for a changing society.* New York: John Wiley & Sons.

Dunn, W. (1997). The impact of sensory processing abilities on the daily lives of young children and their families: A conceptual model. *Infants and Young Children, 9*(4), 23–35.

Fisher, S. D., & Siple, P. (1990). *Theoretical issues in sign language research.* Chicago: University of Chicago Press.

Fleischer, D. A., & Durlach, N. L. (1993). Measuring the dimensions of sensory communication at RLE. *RLE Currents, 6*(2). Retrieved August 18, 2004, from http://rleweb.mit.edu/Publications/currents/6-2cover.htm

Fraiberg, S. (1968). Parallel and divergent patterns in blind and sighted infants. *Psychoanalytic Study of the Child, 23,* 264–300.

Fraiberg, S. (1977). *Insights from the blind.* New York: Basic.

Freeman, P. (1985). *The deaf-blind baby: A programme of care.* London: William Heinnemann Medical Books.

Fuller, D. R., Lloyd, L. L., & Schlosser, R. W. (1992). Further development of an augmentative and alternative communication symbol taxonomy. *Augmentative and Alternative Communication, 8,* 67–74.

Gallagher, N. G. (2003). Effects of infant massage on cognitive, motor, and social-emotional functioning in high-risk infants. *Bridges Practice-Based Research Syntheses, 2* (13), 1–11. Retrieved November 20, 2003, from http://evidencebasedpractices.org

Gibson, J. J. (1962). Observations on active touch. *Psychological Review, 69,* 477–491.

Gibson, J. J. (1966). *The senses considered as perceptual systems.* Boston: Houghton-Mifflin.

Griffith, P. L., & Robinson, J. H. (1980). The influence of iconicity and phonological similarity on sign learning in mentally retarded subjects. *American Journal of Mental Deficiency, 85,* 291–299.

Griffith, P. L., Robinson, J. H., & Panagos, J. H. (1983). Tactile iconicity: Signs related for use with deaf-blind children. *Journal of the Association for Persons with Severe Handicaps, 8*(2) 26–38.

Hagood, L. (n.d.). A standard tactile symbol system: Graphic language for individuals who are blind and unable to learn braille. *SEE/HEAR.* Retrieved March 10, 2005, from www.tsbvi.edu/Outreach/seehear/archive/tactile.html

Harlin, D. (1996). Tactile sign. *TAC News, 8,* 8–11.

Heller, M. A., & Schiff, W. (Eds.) (1991). *The psychology of touch.* Hillsdale, NJ: Lawrence Erlbaum Associates.

Joint, S. (1998). Body signing: A functional strategy for introducing language to students who are deafblind. *Deaf-Blind Review, 21,* 10–11.

Juberg, D. R., Alfano, K., Coughlin, R. J., & Thompson, K. M. (2001). An observational study of object mouthing behavior by young children. *Pediatrics, 107,* 135–142.

Kahn, J. V. (1996). Cognitive skills and sign language knowledge of children with severe and profound mental retardation. *Education and Training in Mental Retardation and Developmental Disabilities, 31,* 162–168.

Kilma, E., & Bellugi, U. (1979). *The signs of language.* Cambridge, MA: Harvard University Press.

Klein, M. D., Chen, D., & Haney, M. (2000). *Promoting learning through active interaction: A guide to early communication with young children who have multiple disabilities.* Baltimore: Paul H. Brookes.

Larrington, G. G. (2002). Sensory integration. In L. Alsop (Ed.), *Understanding deafblindness: Issues, perspectives, and strategies* (Vol. 1, pp. 245–322). Logan, UT: SKI-HI Institute, HOPE.

Lappin, G., & Kretschmer, R. E. (2005). Applying infant massage practices: A qualitative study. *Journal of Visual Impairment & Blindness, 99,* 355–367.

Lederman, S. J., & Klatsky, R. L. (1987). Hand movements: A window into haptic object recognition. *Cognitive Psychology, 19,* 342–368.

Lee, M., & MacWilliam, L. (2002). *Learning together: A creative approach to learning for children with multiple disabilities and a visual impairment.* London: RNIB.

Levack, N. (1994). *Low vision: A resource guide with adaptations for students with visual impairments* (2nd ed.). Austin: Texas School for the Blind and Visually Impaired.

Lewis, S., & Tolla, J. (2003). Creating and using tactile experience books for young children with visual impairments. *TEACHING Exceptional Children, 35*(1), 22–28.

Lynch, E. W., & Hanson, M. J. (2004). *Developing cross-cultural competence: A guide to working with children and their families* (3rd ed.). Baltimore: Paul H. Brookes.

Lynch, S. A., & Simpson, C. G. (2004). Sensory processing: Meeting individual needs using the seven senses. *Young Exceptional Children, 7*(4), 2–9.

MacFarland, S. Z. C. (1995). Teaching strategies of the van Dijk curricular approach. *Journal of Visual Impairment & Blindness, 89,* 222–228.

Maestas Y Moores, J. (1980). Early linguistic environment: Interactions of deaf parents and their infants. *Sign Language Studies, 26,*1–16.

McInnes, J., & Treffry, J. (1982). *Deaf-blind infants and children: A developmental guide.* Buffalo, NY: University of Toronto Press.

McLinden, M. (1999). Hands on: Haptic exploratory strategies in children who are blind with multiple disabilities. *British Journal of Visual Impairment, 17,* 23–29.

McLinden, M. (2004). Haptic exploratory strategies and children who are blind and have additional disabilities. *Journal of Visual Impairment & Blindness, 98,* 99–115.

McLinden, M., & McCall, S. (2002). *Learning through touch: Supporting children with visual impairment and additional difficulties.* London: David Fulton Publishers.

Miles, B. (2002). Touch. In L. Alsop (Ed.), *Understanding deafblindness: Issues, perspectives, and strategies* (Vol. 1, pp. 199–243). Logan, UT: SKI-HI Institute, HOPE.

Miles, B. (2003). Talking the language of the hands to the hands. *Deaf-Blind Link, The National Information Clearinghouse on Children who are Deaf-Blind.* Retrieved March 10, 2005, from http://www.dblink.org/lib/hands.htm

Miles, B., & Riggio, M. (1999). *Remarkable conversations. A guide to developing meaningful conversations with children and young adults who are deafblind.* Watertown, MA: Perkins School for the Blind.

Mirenda, P. (2005). Augmentative and alternative communication techniques. In J. Downing (Ed.), *Teaching communication skills to students with severe disabilities* (2nd ed., pp. 89–112). Baltimore: Paul H. Brookes.

Mizuko, M. (1987). Transparency and ease of learning of symbols represented by Blissymbolics, PCS, and Picsyms. *Augmentative and Alternative Communication, 3,* 129–136.

Montagu, A. (1986). *Touching: The human significance of the skin* (3rd ed.). New York: Harper & Row.

Morange-Majoux, F., Cougnot, P., & Bloch, H. (1997). Hand tactual exploration of textures in infants from 4 to 6 months. *Early Development and Parenting, 6,* 127–135.

Murray-Branch, J., & Bailey, B. R. (1998). *Textures as communication symbols*. Terre Haute: Indiana State University, Blumberg Center for Interdisciplinary Studies in Special Education.

Murray-Branch, J., Udvari-Solner, A., & Bailey, B. (1991). Textured communication systems for individuals with severe intellectual and dual sensory impairments. *Language, Speech, and Hearing Sciences in Schools, 22*, 260–268.

Nielsen, L. (1991). Spatial relations in congenitally blind infants: A study. *Journal of Visual Impairments & Blindness, 85*, 11–18.

No Child Left Behind Act of 2001, Pub.L. No. 107–110, 115 Stat. 1425 (2002).

O'Neill, R. E., Horner, R. H., Albin, R. W., Sprague, J. R., Storey, K., & Newton, J. S. (1997). *Functional assessment and program development for problem behavior: A practical handbook* (2nd ed.). Pacific Grove, CA: Brooks/Cole Thomson Learning.

Palmer, C. F. (1989). The discriminating nature of infant's exploratory actions. *Developmental Psychology, 25*, 885–893.

Pardew, E. M., & Bunse, C. (2005). Enhancing interaction through positive touch. *Young Exceptional Children, 8*(2), 21–29.

Petitto, L. A., & Marentette, P. F. (1991). Babbling in the manual mode: Evidence for the ontogeny of language. *Science, 251*, 1493–1496.

Prickett, J. G. (1995). Manual and spoken language. In K. M. Huebner, J. G. Prickett, T. R. Welch, & E. Joffee (Eds.), *Hand in hand: Essentials of communication and orientation and mobility for your students who are deaf-blind* (pp. 261–286). New York: AFB Press.

Prickett, J. G., & Welch, T. R. (1995). Deaf-blindness: Implications for learning. In K. M. Huebner, J. G. Prickett, T. R. Welch, & E. Joffee (Eds.), *Hand in hand: Essentials of communication and orientation and mobility for your students who are deaf-blind* (pp. 25–60). New York: AFB Press.

Rogow, S. (1987). The ways of the hand: Hand function in blind, visually impaired and visually impaired multihandicapped children. *British Journal of Visual Impairment, 5*(2), 59–62.

Rowland, C. (1996). *Communication matrix*. Portland: Oregon Health Sciences University, Center on Self-Determination.

Rowland, C., & Schweigert, P. (1997). *Home inventory of problem solving skills.* Portland: Oregon Health Sciences University, Center on Self-Determination.

Rowland, C., & Schweigert, P. (2000). Tangible symbols, tangible outcomes. *AAC Augmentative and Alternative Communication, 16,* 61–78.

Rowland, C., Schweigert, P., & Prickett, J. G. (1995). Communication systems, devices and modes. In K. M. Huebner, J. G. Prickett, T. R. Welch, & E. Joffee (Eds.). *Hand in hand: Essentials in communication and orientation and mobility for your students who are deaf-blind* (pp. 219–295). New York: AFB Press.

Ruff, H. A. (1984). Infants' manipulative exploration of objects: Effects of age and object characteristics. *Developmental Psychology, 20,* 9–20.

Ruff, H. A., Saltarelli, L. M., Capozoli, M., & Dubiner, K. (1992). The differentiation of activity in infants' exploration of objects. *Developmental Psychology, 28,* 851–861.

Schellingerhout, R., Smithsman, A. W., & Van Galen, G. P. (1997). Exploration of surface textures in congenitally blind infants. *Child: Care, Health, and Development, 23,* 247–264.

Schellingerhout, R., Smithsman, A. W., & Van Galen, G. P. (1998). Haptic object exploration in congenitally blind infants. *Journal of Visual Impairments & Blindness, 92,* 674–678.

Schneider, E. F. (1996). The power of touch: Massage for infants. *Infants and Young Children, 8*(3), 40–55.

Sigafoos, J. (2000). Communication development and aberrant behavior in children with developmental disabilities. *Education and Training in Mental Retardation and Developmental Disabilities, 35* 168–176.

Snell, M. E. (2002). Using dynamic assessment with learners who communicate nonsymbolically. *Augmentative and Alternative Communication, 18,* 163–176.

Snell, M. E. (2003). Applying research to practice: The more pervasive problem? *Research and Practice for Persons with Severe Disabilities, 28,* 143–147.

Spencer, P. E. (2001). *A good start: Suggestions for visual conversations with deaf and hard of hearing babies and toddlers.* Retrieved August 21, 2004, from http://clerccenter2 .gallaudet.edu/KidsWorldDeafNet/e-docs/visual-conversations/index.html

Spencer, P., Bodner-Johnson, B., & Gutfreund, M. (1992). Interacting with infants with a hearing loss: What can we learn from mothers who are deaf? *Journal of Early Intervention, 16,* 64–78.

Texas School for the Blind and Visually Impaired. (n.d.). *Tactile symbols directory to standard tactile symbol list.* Retrieved August 21, 2004, from http://www.tsbvi.edu/Education/vmi/tactile_symbols.htm

Thestrup, A., & Anderson, O. V. (1994). Modified sign language for congenitally deaf-blind people: Ann Thestrup and Ove Vedel Anderson report on developments in Denmark. *Deaf-Blind Education, 13,* 16–17.

van Dijk, J. (1966). The first steps of the deaf-blind child toward language. *International Journal of the Education of the Blind, 15,* 112–114.

van Dijk, J. (1986). An educational curriculum for deaf-blind multihandicapped persons. In D. Ellis (Ed.), *Sensory impairment in mentally handicapped people* (pp. 374–383). London, England: Croom-Helm.

Venkatagiri, H. S. (2002). Clinical implications of an augmentative and alternative communication taxonomy. *Augmentative and Alternative Communication, 18,* 45–57.

Vernon, M., & Andrews, J. A. (1990). *The psychology of deafness.* Reading, MA: Addison Wesley Longman.

Warren, D. H. (1994). *Blindness and children: An individual differences approach.* New York: Cambridge University Press.

Watkins, S., & Clark, T. C. (1991). A coactive sign system for children who are dual-sensory impaired. *American Annals of the Deaf, 136,* 321–324.

Westling, D. L., & Fox, L. (2004). *Teaching students with severe disabilities* (3rd ed.). Upper Saddle River, NJ: Merrill.

Williamson, G. G., & Anzalone, M. E. (2001). *Sensory integration and regulation in infants and toddlers: Helping very young children interact with their environment.* Washington, DC: Zero to Three.

Wolf, M. M. (1978). Social validity: The case for subjective measurement, or how applied behavior analysis is finding its heart. *Journal of Applied Behavior Analysis, 11,* 203–214.

Wormsley, D. P. (1997). Fostering emergent literacy. In D. P. Wormsley and F. M. D'Andrea (Eds.), *Instructional strategies for braille efficiency* (pp. 17–56). New York: AFB Press.

Wormsley, D. P. (2004). *Braille literacy: A functional approach.* New York: AFB Press.

Resources

SOURCES OF INFORMATION

Organizations

American Foundation for the Blind (AFB)

11 Penn Plaza, Suite 300
New York, NY 10001
(212) 502–7600 or (800) 232–5463
TDD: (212) 502–7662
Fax: (212) 502–7777
E-mail: afbinfo@afb.net
www.afb.org

A national organization serving as an information clearinghouse for people who are blind or visually impaired and their families, professionals, organizations, schools, and corporations. Mounts program initiatives to improve services to persons with visual impairment in such areas as aging, education, employment, literacy, and technology; conducts research and advocates for services and legislation; maintains the M. C. Migel Library and Information Center and the Helen Keller Archives; provides information and referral services; and produces videos and publishes books, journals, and other materials.

American Printing House for the Blind (APH)

P.O. Box 6085
1839 Frankfort Avenue
Louisville, KY 40206–0085
(502) 895–2405 or (800) 223–1839
(502) 899–2274
E-mail: info@aph.org
www.aph.org

A publisher of books, producer of braille and other accessible materials, and manufacturer of educational tools and daily living products for individuals of all ages who are blind or visually impaired.

Association for Education and Rehabilitation of the Blind and Visually Impaired (AER)

1703 N. Beauregard Street, Suite 440
Alexandria, VA 22311
(703) 671–4500 or (877) 492–2708
Fax: (703) 671–6391
E-mail: aer@aerbvi.org
www.aerbvi.org

A professional membership organization that promotes all phases of education and work for persons of all ages who are blind and visually impaired. Has 17 divisions, including one that addresses the educational needs of infants and preschoolers, another that focuses on the needs of students with multiple disabilities, and an orientation and mobility division. Organizes conferences and workshops, maintains job-exchange services and a speakers' bureau, holds continuing education seminars, and is involved in legislative and advocacy projects. Publishes *RE:view,* a quarterly journal, and *AER Reports,* a newsletter, and has state or regional chapters in the United States and Canada.

Closing the Gap

526 Main Street
P.O. Box 68
Henderson, MN 56044
(507) 248–3294
Fax: (507) 248–3810
www.closingthegap.com

A source for information on assistive technology resources for children and adults with disabilities through its bi-monthly newspaper, annual international conference, and print and online resource directory.

Council for Exceptional Children (CEC)

1110 North Glebe Road, Suite 300
Arlington, VA 22201–5704
(703) 620–3660 or (888) 221–6830
Fax: (703) 264–9494
TDD: (866) 915–5000
E-mail: service@cec.sped.org
www.cec.sped.org

A professional organization for teachers, school administrators, and others working to improve educational outcomes for students with exceptionalities, including those with disabilities or who are gifted. Advocates for newly and historically underserved individuals with exceptionalities and for appropriate governmental policies, sets professional standards, provides continual professional development, and helps professionals obtain conditions and resources necessary for effective professional practice.

DB-LINK—The National Information Clearinghouse on Children Who Are Deaf-Blind

345 North Monmouth Avenue
Monmouth, OR 97361
(800) 438–9376
TDD: (800) 854–7013
Fax: (503) 838–8150
E-mail: dblink@tr.wou.edu
www.dblink.org

A federally funded clearinghouse that provides online information on deaf-blindness, including contacts for state and national agencies, articles, full text publications, Internet resources, and a database. Publishes the newsletter *Deaf-Blind Perspectives*.

National Dissemination Center for Children with Disabilities (NICHCY)

P.O. Box 1492
Washington, DC 20013

(800) 695–0285
Fax: (202) 884–8441
E-mail: nichcy@aed.org
www.nichcy.org

A federally funded center providing information on disabilities in children of all ages, the Individuals with Disabilities Education Improvement Act, No Child Left Behind legislation, and research-based information on effective educational practices.

National Early Childhood Technical Assistance Center (NECTAC)

Campus Box 8040—UNC Chapel Hill
Chapel Hill, NC 27599–8040
(919) 962–7324
Fax: (919) 966–7463
TDD: (919) 843–3269
www.nectas.unc.edu

An organization providing a rich variety of resources related to early intervention and early childhood special education, including listings of state Part C and Section 619 coordinators, federally funded projects, topic pages related to the implementation of the early childhood provisions of the Individuals with Disabilities Education Improvement Act, and bibliographies.

National Institute on Deafness and Other Communication Disorders (NIDCD)

National Institutes of Health
31 Center Drive, MSC 2320
Bethesda, MD 20892–2320
(301) 496–7243
TDD: (301) 402–0252
www.nidcd.nih.gov

An institute of the National Institutes of Health within the U.S. Department of Health and Human Services that supports and conducts research and research training on health topics related to hearing, ear infections and deafness; voice, speech, and language; and related subjects.

TASH (formerly The Association for Persons with Severe Handicaps)

29 West Susquehanna Avenue, Suite 210
Baltimore, MD 21204
(410) 828–8274
Fax: (410) 828–6706
E-mail: info@tash.org
www.tash.org

An international association of people with disabilities, their family members, other advocates, and professionals. Offers conferences and print and online resources on issues related to people with disabilities and their families.

Texas School for the Blind and Visually Impaired (TSBVI)

1100 West 45th Street
Austin, TX 78756–3494
(512) 454–8631 or (800) 872–5273
Fax: (512) 454–3395
TDD: (512) 206–9188
www.tsbvi.edu

A special school and learning and outreach center that is a source of extensive information about working with children who are blind or visually impaired, including professional publications, assessments, and curricula, much of it available online.

Web Sites

American Sign Language Browser

http://commtechlab.msu.edu/sites/aslweb/browser.htm
Easy-to-use online ASL dictionary with a video to demonstrate each sign.

Circle of Inclusion

www.circleofinclusion.org

Offers demonstrations of and information about effective practices of inclusive early childhood programs for children from birth to 8 years of age.

CLAS (Culturally and Linguistically Appropriate Services) Early Childhood Research Institute

http://clas.uiuc.edu

Provides online reviews of early childhood special education books, videos, curricula, and other materials and their relevance to families and children of diverse cultural and linguistic backgrounds.

Educational Resources Information Center/ERIC Project

www.eric.ed.gov

Provides an online database of journal and nonjournal education literature, sponsored by the Institute of Education Sciences (IES) of the U.S. Department of Education.

Family Village

www.familyvillage.wisc.edu

Offers an organized directory of online resources on a variety of issues related to persons with cognitive and other disabilities including specific diagnoses, adaptive equipment and technology, recreation, education, health issues, disability-related media, and literature.

Inclusion

www.uni.edu/coe/inclusion/index.html

Provides answers to questions regarding inclusive education for children with disabilities for general and special education teachers, school staff, and families.

Kids Together

www.kidstogether.org

Provides information and a forum on educating children with disabilities in general education settings.

National Parent Information Network

http://npin.org

Provides information for parents of older school-aged children with disabilities on a variety of topics including homework, learning disabilities, applied behavioral analysis, and pervasive developmental disorders.

National Parent Network on Disabilities

www.npnd.org

Provides information on a variety of topics, including emotional problems, attention deficit disorder, and schizophrenia.

Parents Helping Parents

www.php.com

Provides online resource information and support for parents of children with special needs.

Project SALUTE (Successful Adaptations for Learning to Use Touch Effectively)

www.projectsalute.net

Provides online information sheets on tactile strategies, including mutual tactile attention, hand-under-hand guidance, touch and object cues, textured symbols, and adapted signs.

SPARKLE (Supporting Parent Access to Resources, Knowledge, Linkages, and Education)

www.sparkle.usu.edu

Provides training for parents of children who are deaf-blind through DVDs and the Internet.

Special Education Resources on the Internet (SERI)

http://seriweb.com

Provides a collection of online resources in the field of special education.

SOURCES OF ASSISTIVE AND EDUCATIONAL PRODUCTS

AbleNet

> 2808 Fairview Avenue North
> Roseville, MN 55113–1308
> (800) 322–0956
> (651) 294–2200 (outside U.S.)
> Fax: (651) 294–2259
> www.ablenetinc.com

Provides assistive technology products for teaching children with disabilities.

Assistive Technology

> 333 Elm Street
> Dedham, MA 02026
> (781) 461–8200 or (800) 793–9227
> Fax: (781) 461–8213
> www.assistivetech.com

Develops and provides hardware and software programs for individuals with physical, cognitive, and speech disabilities.

Design to Learn Projects

> 707 S.W. Gaines Road
> Portland, OR 97239
> (503) 494–2619 or (888) 909–4030
> Fax: (503) 494–2859
> E-mail: design@ohsu.edu
> www.designtolearn.com

Develops effective assessment and teaching strategies for children and adults with low-incidence disabilities. Conducts training for teachers, speech-language pathologists, and other professionals. Also offers college courses for students in fields related to special education.

DynaVox Systems

> 2100 Wharton Street, Suite 400
> Pittsburgh, PA 15203
> (412) 381–4883 or (866) 396–2869
> Fax: (412) 381–5241
> www.dynavoxsys.com

Develops and provides augmentative communication devices for individuals with disabilities.

Enabling Devices: Toys for Special Children

> 385 Warburton Avenue
> Hastings-on-Hudson, NY 10706
> (914) 478–0960 or (800) 832–8697
> Fax: (914) 479–1369
> E-mail: info@enablingdevices.com
> www.enablingdevices.com

Offers assistive devices for children.

IntelliTools

> 1720 Corporate Circle
> Petaluma, CA 94954
> (707) 773–2000 or (800) 899–6687
> Fax: (707) 773–2001
> E-mail: info@intellitools.com
> www.intellitools.com

Designs products for students who face challenges ranging from learning disabilities to significant physical disabilities, including IntelliKeys, an alternative keyboard for children with physical, visual, and cognitive disabilities. Develops curriculum software to help students meet national and state standards in math and language arts.

Mayer Johnson

P.O. Box 1579
Solana Beach, CA 92075–7579
(858) 550–0084 or (800) 588–4548
Fax: (858) 550–0449
www.mayer-johnson.com

Develops and provides easy-to-use communication tools and software for individuals with disabilities.

Prentke Romich Company

1022 Heyl Road
Wooster, OH 44691
(330) 262–1984 or (800) 262–1984
Fax: (330) 263–4829
E-mail: info@prentrom.com
www.prentrom.com

Develops and provides a variety of augmentative communication devices.

R. J. Cooper & Associates

Software and Hardware for Persons with Special Needs
27601 Forbes Road, Suite 39
Laguna Niguel, CA 92677
(949) 582–2572 or (800) 752–6673
Fax: (949) 582–3169
E-mail: info@rjcooper.com
www.rjcooper.com

Develops and provides software and hardware adaptations for individuals with disabilities.

TACK-TILES Braille System

P.O. Box 475
Plaistow, NH 03865
(603) 382–1904 or (800) 822–5845
Fax: (603) 382–1748
www.tack-tiles.com

Manufactures TACK-TILES Braille System, a teaching tool for teaching braille based on Lego-type blocks.

Technology Integration

Linda Burkhart
6201 Candle Court
Eldersburg, MD 21784
Fax: (410) 795–8834
E-mail: linda@lburkhart.com
www.lburkhart.com

Provides online resources on assistive technology and augmentative communication, using the Internet in elementary and middle schools, and other related products.

SELECTED READINGS

Aitken, S., Buultjens, M., Clark, C., Eyre, J. T., & Pease, L. (2000). *Teaching children who are deafblind: Contact, communication and learning.* London: David Fulton.

A discussion of deaf-blindness and the need for strategies for promoting a child's communication and social interaction. Provides information on assessment, instruction, and curriculum.

Alsop, L. (Ed.). (2002). *Understanding deafblindness: Issues, perspectives and strategies.* Logan, UT: HOPE.

A two-volume comprehensive resource for working with children who are deaf-blind. Includes chapters on communication and ways to promote a child's use of touch and tactile information.

Barnard, K. E., & Brazelton, T. B. (Eds.). (1990). *Touch: The foundation of experience* (Rev. and expanded ed.). Guilford, CT: International Universities Press.

A discussion of tactile experiences from philosophical, neuroanatomical, developmental, and therapeutic perspectives from proceedings of the Johnson and Johnson Pediatric Round Table X.

Blaha, R. (2001). *Calendars for students with multiple impairments including deafblindness: A systematic process supporting communication, time and emotional being.* Austin: Texas School for the Blind and Visually Impaired.

A step-by-step guide that describes the benefits of calendar systems and provides information on the continuum of different types of calendars and on how to develop them. Also available in Spanish.

Chen, D. (Ed.). (1999). *Essential elements in early intervention: Visual impairments and multiple disabilities.* New York: AFB Press.

A guide that focuses on supports for infants who have visual impairments and multiple disabilities. Chapters are organized under three areas—the principles of early intervention, vision and hearing assessment, and the development of learning strategies. Includes explanations of functional and clinical vision and hearing assessments, descriptions of evaluative and educational techniques, and suggestions on working effectively with families.

Chen, D., & Dote-Kwan, J. (Eds). (1995). *Starting points: Instructional practices for young children whose multiple disabilities include visual impairment.* Los Angeles: Blind Childrens Center.

A manual that provides a framework and specific strategies for teaching young children with visual impairments and additional disabilities. Topics include identifying characteristics and learning needs, guiding principles for instruction, instructional strategies, communication, daily living skills, positive behavior support, orientation and mobility, occupational therapy, roles of itinerant teachers, and family perspectives.

Downing, J. E. (2002). *Including students with severe and multiple disabilities in typical classrooms: Practical strategies for teachers* (2nd ed.) Baltimore: Paul H. Brookes.

A resource for educators that covers the age span from preschool through high school of students in typical settings. Provides examples of students with multiple disabilities, including sensory and deaf-blindness. Specific strategies target ways of fully including all students in the learning process despite very complex and challenging needs. Considerable attention is paid to adapting academic areas and providing practical suggestions.

Downing, J. E. (2005). *Teaching communication skills to students with severe disabilities* (2nd ed.). Baltimore: Paul H. Brookes.

A guide that offers many practical strategies for assessing the communication skills of students with very complex and challenging needs. A student-centered and natural context approach is taken in determining what communication skills are needed. Suggestions are provided for facilitating development of communication skills in everyday situations across the age span and multiple modes of communication are stressed.

Downing, J. E. (2005). *Teaching literacy to students with significant disabilities: Strategies for the K-12 inclusive classroom.* Thousand Oaks, CA: Corwin Press.

A manual that stresses the importance of literacy for all children and specifically focuses on those who have often been denied access to literacy experiences. The concept of literacy is defined broadly to enable access for all children. Specific examples of adapted literacy materials and activities at different age and grade levels are provided throughout the text.

Durkel, J. (1999). *Non-verbal communication: Cues, signals and symbols* [Online]. Available: http://www.tsbvi.edu/Education/vmi/nonverbal.htm

A factsheet that defines the difference between cues, signals, and symbols.

Hagood, L. (1997). *Communication: A guide to teaching students with visual and multiple impairments.* Austin: Texas School for the Blind and Visually Impaired.

A discussion of how deaf-blindness and visual impairment in children with severe disabilities can affect their communication. Provides approaches for assessing and teaching communication skills and describes a standard tactual symbol system and reproducible forms.

Harrell, L. (1984). *Touch the baby: Blind and visually impaired children as patients. Helping them respond to care.* New York: AFB Press.

Practical information on the use of communication and touch cues in clinical settings. These signals help young children to understand when interactions will involve caregiving or comfort, and when they will involve uncomfortable medical procedures.

Huebner, K. M., Prickett, J. G. Welch, T. R., & Joffe, E. (Eds.). (1995). *Hand in hand: Essentials of communication and orientation and mobility for your students who are deaf-blind.* New York: AFB Press.

A comprehensive resource that provides information on communication and orientation and mobility instruction for students who are deaf-blind. Provides key concepts, instructional strategies, and learning activities for working on these two areas with preschoolers, elementary, and high school students who are deaf-blind.

Klein, M. D., Chen, D., & Haney, M. (2000). *Promoting learning through active interaction. A guide to early communication with young children who have multiple disabilities.* Baltimore: Paul H. Brookes.

A field-tested curriculum composed of five modules for promoting intentional communication with young children who have severe and multiple disabilities. Handouts and recording sheets are provided in English and Spanish.

Lee, M., & MacWilliam, L. (2002). *Learning together. A creative approach to learning for children with multiple disabilities and a visual impairment.* London: RNIB.

A description of a communication program that has been used extensively with children who have multiple disabilities and visual impairment in Scotland. Topics include movement interaction, developing natural gesture, learning a sign system, encouraging play, the learning environment, and observations of nonverbal communication.

McLinden, M., & McCall, S. (2002). *Learning through touch. Supporting children with visual impairment and additional difficulties.* London: David Fulton.

Provides an in-depth discussion of research on the sense of touch and the influence of visual impairment and additional disabilities on learning through touch. Offers practical suggestions for assessing a child's use of touch and for developing learning experiences, communication, early literacy, and tactile symbols.

Miles, B. (2003). *Talking the language of the hands to the hands: The importance of hands for the person who is deafblind* (Rev.). [Online]. Available: http://www.dblink.org/lib/hands.htm

Information focusing on the development of social relationships and language through hand movements, manual exploration, and tactile interactions with children who are deaf-blind. Provides strategies on ways to initiate and maintain interactions with children who are deaf-blind. Available in English, Spanish, German, and Swedish.

Miles, B. (2005). Literacy for persons who are deaf-blind (Rev ed.). [Online]. Available: http://www.dblink.org/lib/literacy.htm

A discussion of the various aspects of literacy as important for individuals who are deaf-blind. These include the social functions of reading and writing, conditions that facilitate literacy, and how to make literacy materials accessible to individuals who are deaf-blind.

Miles, B., & McLetchie, B. (2004). *Developing concepts with children who are deaf-blind.* [Online]. Available: http://www.dblink.org/lib/concepts.htm

An overview of the influence of deaf-blindness on concept development. Emphasizes the importance of relationships, communication and conversation, access to the world, and activities and routines in supporting concept development in children who are deaf-blind.

Miles, B., & Riggio, M. (Eds.). (1999). *Remarkable conversations: A guide to developing meaningful conversations with children and young adults who are deafblind.* Watertown, MA: Perkins School for the Blind.

A manual that addresses the complexity of communication with students who are deaf-blind and who demonstrate different levels of ability. Contains photographs of interactions with these students. Topics include understanding deaf-blindness, conversations as the essence of communication, partnerships with families, selection of communication modes, developing language, and meeting the needs of individuals.

Montagu, A. (1986). *Touching. The human significance of the skin* (3rd ed.). New York: Harper & Row.

A discussion of the profound effects of tactile experiences on emotion, behavior, and development. Draws on diverse studies of animals and humans from the fields of medicine, biology, psychology, and anthropology to demonstrate the importance of tactile stimulation and physical contact.

Rowland, C., & Schweigert, P. (2000). *Tangible symbol systems* (rev. ed.). Portland, OR: Design to Learn Projects.

A manual that provides a field-tested systematic instructional sequence for teaching students who have severe and multiple disabilities to communicate using a concrete symbol system. Tangible symbols (objects or pictures) are defined as having an obvious relationship to their referents.

Rowland, C., & Schweigert, P. (2005). *First things first. Early communication for the presymbolic child with severe disabilities.* Portland, OR: Design to Learn Projects.

A manual that provides an overview of communication development, with a focus on strategies to support children who are pre-symbolic communicators. Offers a format for assessing the child's communicative behaviors and for collecting data to monitor and evaluate intervention.

Smith, M. (Summer, 1998). Feelin' groovy: Functional tactual skills. *See/Hear, 3*(3). Available: http://www.tsbvi.edu/Outreach/seehear/summer98/groovy.htm

Strategies for supporting tactile skills during interactions with children who have visual impairments and multiple disabilities. Provides a format for observing and identifying the child's tactile skills within daily activities and many practical suggestions. Available in English and Spanish.

OTHER MATERIALS

Assessment Tools

Rowland, C. (1996). *Communication matrix. A communication skill assessment for individuals at the earliest stages of communication development.* Portland, OR: Design to Learn Projects.

Identifies the range of communication development from pre-intentional and intentional behaviors to the use of abstract symbols and language.

Rowland, C., & Schweigert, P. (1997). *Home inventory of problem solving skills.* Portland, OR: Design to Learn Projects.

Focuses on early cognitive development of nonverbal children who have severe and multiple disabilities. Used to assess a child's basic skills with objects, ways the child gains access to objects, and ways he or she uses objects.

Videos

Chen, D., & Downing, J. (2006). *Tactile learning strategies: Interacting with children who have visual impairments and multiple disabilities.* [Video and DVD]. New York, AFB Press.

Shows examples of a number of tactile strategies, including mutual tactile attention, tactile modeling, hand-under-hand and hand-over-hand guidance, touch and object cues, and coactive and tactile signing. Available in English and Spanish (closed-captioned).

Chen, D., Klein, M. D., & Haney, M. (2000). *Promoting learning through active interaction: An instructional video.* [Video and booklet]. Baltimore: Paul H. Brookes.

Demonstrates a step-by-step process for developing intentional communication with young children with severe and multiple disabilities. Available in English (closed-captioned) and Spanish.

Chen, D., & Schachter, P. H. (1997). *Making the most of early communication. Strategies for supporting communication with infants, toddlers, and preschoolers whose multiple disabilities include vision and hearing loss.* [Video and booklet]. New York: AFB Press.

Provides examples of early caregiver-infant games, simulations of visual impairment and hearing loss, and strategies to promote communication in young children. Includes interviews with parents and teachers and preschoolers in oral and total communication classrooms. Available with closed captions and audio description.

Cooley, E. (1987). *Getting in touch.* [Video and booklet]. Champaign, IL: Research Press.

Demonstrates the use of touch and object cues with children of a wide age range who are deaf-blind. Also provides tips on interpersonal and tactile considerations in greeting, and interacting with a student who is totally deaf and blind.

Hands on experience: Tactual learning skills. [Can Do! video series]. (1996). Louisville, KY: Visually Impaired Preschool Services.

Demonstrates the benefits of touching, handling, and manipulating objects, and active participation in everyday situations. For children who are blind, these hands-on experiences provide the foundation for braille reading.

Huebner, K. M., Prickett, J. G., Welch, T. R., & Joffe, E. (Eds.). (1995). *Hand in hand: It can be done.* [Video and booklet]. New York: AFB Press.

Provides an introduction to working with students of all ages who are deaf-blind, with a particular focus on communication and orientation and mobility. Includes demonstrations of practical suggestions and insights from teachers and family members. Available with closed captions.

Murray-Branch, J., & Bailey, B. (1997). *Textured communication symbols: Talking through touch*. [Video and booklet]. Terre Haute, IN: Blumberg Center for Interdisciplinary Studies in Special Education, Indiana State University.

Provides considerations for developing a communication system using textures for individuals with multiple disabilities and sensory impairments. Offers guidelines for deciding whether an individual needs textured symbols and how to develop them. A four-phase instructional process is provided to teach an individual to use the communication system.

Rowland, C., & Schweigert, P. (1996). *Tangible symbol systems* (Rev. ed.). [Video]. Portland, OR: Design to Learn Projects.

Provides illustrations of individuals using tangible symbols and shows how five children learned to use this system of communication. Companion video to the manual *Tangible Symbol Systems* (2000).

SKI-HI Institute. (1990). *A coactive sign system.* [Video series]. Logan, UT: HOPE.

Demonstrates how to use coactive signing with children who need this hand-on-hand system of communication. Provides vocabulary and teaching tips, and shows the use of coactive signs in home situations. A series of nine closed-captioned videotapes.

SKI-HI Institute. (1992–93). *Introduction to tactile communication series.* [Video]. Logan, UT: HOPE.

A closed-captioned videotape that introduces tactile communication and the other videotapes in the series on tactile communication.

SKI-HI Institute. (1992–93). *Using tactile interactive conversational signing.* [Video series]. Logan, UT: HOPE.

Demonstrates the use of interactive signing (feeling another's signs), the transition from coactive to interactive signing, materials and activities that promote interaction, supporting interaction with peers, and interpreting for people who use interactive signs. A series of five closed-captioned videotapes.

SKI-HI Institute. (1993). *Using tactile signals and cues.* [Video series]. Logan, UT: HOPE.

Demonstrates how to use tactile signals and cues with young children who need tactile communication. Illustrates specific strategies for selecting and using signals, providing choices, promoting turn-taking, using coactive signs, and creating activities to support communication. A series of five close-captioned videotapes.

Where do I begin? Developing communication with children who are born deafblind. [Video]. (2001). Maylands, West Australia: West Australia Deafblind Association.

Presents key strategies for developing communication with children who are deaf-blind: Making contact "approach," building rapport, acknowledging communication efforts, using tactile cues and symbols, tactile signing, establishing routines, choice-making, and interrupted routine. Stresses the importance of following the child's lead, particularly following the child's hands in supporting expressive communication, respecting the child's needs and consistent use of selected communication system.

You & Me. Communication. [Video]. (1994). Monmouth, OR: Teaching Research Division, Western Oregon State College.

Provides information on the concepts, skills, and supports that are needed for a student who is deaf-blind to communicate in an inclusive elementary school. Demonstrates the use of object cues, coactive signing, and tactile signing with adults and peers. Available with open captions.

Glossary

Adapted sign: Modification of a standard manual sign to fit the child's visual, cognitive, and motor abilities, or to accommodate for the child's visual impairment or learning needs.

American Sign Language (ASL): The natural language of deaf people belonging to Deaf culture in the United States, consisting of manual signs and other movements, including body postures and facial expressions. It has its own grammatical rules and structure that are different from the rules of English.

CHARGE: A diagnostic label of a pattern of genetic anomalies that may include coloboma, heart defect, choneal atresia, retarded growth and development, genital hypoplasia, and anomalies or malformation of the ears and hearing loss.

Coactive movement: Based on the work of Jan van Dijk, coactive movement is defined as moving together with the child. The adult or peer performs movements (which may include objects) concurrently with the child.

Coactive signing: Physical guidance of a child's hand or hands to facilitate production of a standard manual sign for expressive communication.

Discrepancy analysis: Determining the possible cause for the difference in the performance (level of skill and behaviors) of a child with a disability and that of a child without a disability in a particular activity.

Ecological inventory: Listing of a sequence of steps in a selected activity and environment in a child's day.

Hand-over-hand guidance: Physically guiding a child's hand or hands through an action or activity.

Hand-under-hand guidance: Placing a hand or hands under a child's hand or hands to allow the child to "see" your hands and what you are doing or touching and to provide the child with access to the environment.

Haptic perception: Active exploration by touch of an object's size, shape, or texture that results in its identification.

Hierarchy of prompts: Sequence of actions that are intended to assist a child in initiating a response, arranged in order of how much assistance is offered, from most to least or from least to most.

Home sign: Idiosyncratic gestures (not based on standard manual signs) that have been developed by a family of a child who is deaf.

Hypotonia: Low muscle tone.

Iconic sign: A manual sign that resembles the object or activity that it represents (for example, COMB and WASH).

IEP: Individualized Education Program

IFSP: Individualized Family Service Plan

Interactive signing: Use of signs involving a sender and receiver in conversational interaction.

Joint attention: Process of sharing experience of an object or event with another through gaze or pointing to indicate the focus of attention.

Mutual tactile attention: Process of giving joint attention to and sharing an activity or object through noncontrolling mutual touch.

Object cue: An object or part of an object used to represent a person, place, object, or activity. This object may be used in the actual situation.

Object of reference: An object or part of an object used to represent a person, place, object, or activity. This object is not used in the actual situation.

Prompt: An act or cue that helps a child to initiate a response.

Sensory integration: Organization and processing of sensory information

Sensory modulation: Ability to manage one's reactions to sensory input.

Signs: Words in ASL that are conveyed by a system of articulated hand shapes, movements, placements, and orientations.

Signs on body: A standard manual sign that a signer produces directly onto the receiver's body. Also known as "body-based signs" and "body signs."

Somatosensory: Relating to sensory information as perceived by the skin (including receptors that perceive pain, temperature, light touch, pressure, and vibration).

Symbol: Something that represents something else. A symbol may be abstract (for example, a spoken or printed word) or closely related to its referent (for example, an object or iconic manual sign).

Tactile: Related to the sense of touch or act of touching. Synonymous with *tactual*.

Tactile discrimination: The ability to perceive similarities and differences of various stimuli to the skin, either when touching objects or when being touched by someone or something.

Tactile learning: The use of tactile information for interaction and to develop conceptual skills.

Tactile hyperreactivity: An increased or heightened sensitivity to tactile stimulation, characterized by observable negative behavioral responses to certain types of tactile stimuli that most people would not find aversive. Also known as tactile defensiveness.

Tactile hyporeactivity: Decreased awareness or sensitivity to tactile stimulation that results in a lack of response or muted response.

Tactile modeling: Demonstration of an activity by having the child or observer feel the demonstrator's actions by touching parts of the body and objects involved in the action.

Tactile saliency: Distinctive physical or tactile characteristics of an item that make it easy to discriminate through touch.

Tactile signing: Communication method based on a standard manual sign system in which the receiver's hand or hands are placed lightly upon the hand or hands of the signer to perceive the signs tactilely.

Tactile strategies: A variety of planned and systematic techniques that include ways of interacting (such as mutual tactile attention, tactile modeling, hand-under-hand guidance, and hand-over-hand guidance) and communicating (such as touch and object cues, textured symbols, and adapted signs) with the child using touch.

Tadoma: Vibrotactile communication method in which a receiver of communication who is deaf-blind places a hand or hands on the speaker's face to perceive what is being said.

Tangible symbols: A communication system that includes three-dimensional symbols (objects) and two-dimensional symbols (photographs and drawings) for children who do not understand the meaning of abstract symbols. Rowland and Schweigert (2000) include photos and drawings because they are permanent, can be touched and manipulated, and have a perceptual link to their referents.

Textured symbols: Tactilely salient, three-dimensional, and artificial representations associated with people, objects, and activities and used for receptive and expressive communication. These symbols can be abstract or closely related to their referent.

Touch cue: A physical prompt made in a consistent manner directly on the body to communicate with a child.

Index

A

Accommodations, 60, 62, 148

Active touch, 5, 16–17, 19–25, 27
   exploratory procedures, 21
   identifying opportunities for, 22–23
   versus passive touch, 17, 22–23, 24
   in sighted infants, 19–20
   in simulation activity, 27
   in visually impaired children, 20–21
   in visually impaired children with additional disabilities, 21, 27

Activities
   analysis of, 62–63
   daily, and multiple tactile strategies, 22, 43, 55, 58, 74
   See also Simulation activities

Adaptation of visual material to tactile mode, 3, 4

Adapted signs, 11, 120–121, 122, 126, 130, 137, 144

Adaptive devices, 1

American Sign Language (ASL), 12, 96, 119, 127, 130, 144
   acquisition of signs, 119–120
   cognitive functioning requirements for, 120
   inaccessibility for children with vision and hearing loss, 127
   modifications and interference with communication, 130
   See also Signing

Assessment, 36, 45, 55, 57–62, 66, 72, 150
   dynamic, 58
   ecological, 36, 57–58, 63, 64–65, 66, 72, 144
      and discrepancy analysis example, 12, 46, 57–58, 60–61
   hierarchy of prompts, 66
   See also Activities, analysis of; Intervention; Interviews

Assistance, least to most, 68–69

Auditory cue, 69, 71, 72

Awareness and attention to materials, 22

B

Bliss, Charles, 96

Blisssymbols, 96–97

Braille, 22, 23, 63, 86, 89, 95, 160, 162, 163, 164
   and literacy promotion, 163–165
   recognition of , 22

C

Challenges. *See* Teaching

CHARGE syndrome, 7

Coactive signing, 8, 12, 29, 33, 102, 107–109, 125, 126–128, 129, 136, 141, 143, 153
   examples, 136
   and expressive communication, 127
   versus tactile signing, 153
   usage guidelines, 129
   videotape (SKI*HI Institute), 127

About the Authors

Deborah Chen, Ph.D., is a professor in the Department of Special Education, California State University, Northridge, teaching in the Early Childhood Special Education program. She has had extensive experience working with young children who have low-incidence and multiple disabilities and their families as infant specialist, teacher, program administrator, teacher trainer, and researcher. Her research and publications focus on early communication with young children who are deaf-blind, interactions between caregivers and infants who have sensory impairments and multiple disabilities, families of diverse cultural and linguistic backgrounds, and interdisciplinary instruction through distance education. She is the editor of *Essential Elements in Early Intervention: Visual Impairments and Multiple Disabilities* and co-author of *Promoting Learning through Active Interaction: A Guide to Early Communication with Young Children Who Have Multiple Disabilities* and *Working with Children from Diverse Cultural Backgrounds,* among other publications, and has written numerous journal articles and book chapters. Dr. Chen has also produced or co-produced a number of videos demonstrating different aspects of work with young children with disabilities, including *Tactile Learning Strategies: Interacting with Children Who Have Visual Impair-ments and Multiple Disabilities,* the companion to this book; *Making the Most of Early Communication; What Can Baby See?* and *Vision Tests for Infants with Multiple Disabilities; Conversations for Three; Culturally Responsive and Family Focused Training;* and *What Can Baby Hear?*

June E. Downing, Ph.D, is a professor in the Department of Special Education, California State University, Northridge, where she prepares teachers to work in the area of moderate and severe disabilities. Her focus has been on the needs of students with severe and multiple disabilities, especially with regard to inclusive education. She has served as a teacher of students with disabilities, as well as a state, regional, and national consultant in areas of appropriate programming, assessment, communication, and inclusion for students with moderate to profound disabilities. Dr. Downing is on the Executive Board of TASH (formerly the Association for Persons with Severe Handicaps) and is past president of its California chapter, an associate editor of *Research and Practices for Persons with Severe Disabilities,* and on the editorial board of

Augmentative and Alternative Communication, and she has published numerous articles and book chapters and has presented widely. Her books include *Teaching Communication Skills to Students with Severe Disabilities; Teaching Literacy for Students with Significant Disabilities: Strategies for Inclusive K–12 Classrooms;* and *Including Students with Severe and Multiple Disabilities in Typical Settings: Practical Suggestions for Teachers.* She was also co-producer of the companion video to this book, *Tactile Learning Strategies: Interacting with Children Who Have Visual Impairments and Multiple Disabilities.*